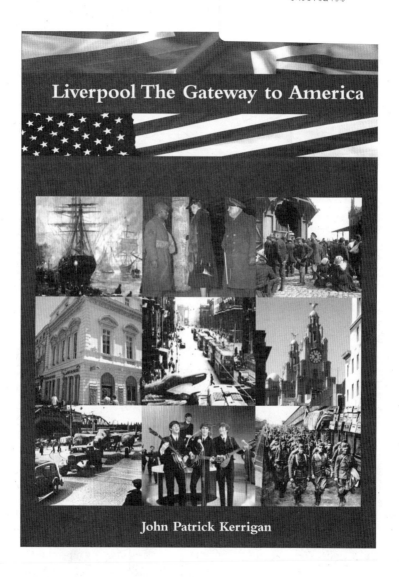

Liverpool The Gateway to America

John Patrick Kerrigan

Published by
AJH Publishing
54 Brows Lane
Formby
L37 4ED

Printed by
Ribcar
56 Lower Breck Road
Tuebrook, Liverpool
L6 4BZ

ISBN 978-0-9554854-3-5

Dedicated with love to my Wife Barbara
Daughters Julie and Laura,
and Grandchildren, Ben, Ciara, Alexandra, and Anya.

Contents

Profile of
John Patrick Kerrigan

Liverpool Author, John Patrick Kerrigan, was born in March 1937 at Walton Hospital in North Liverpool.

He was just two years old when World War Two started, but he still maintains that it had very little to do with him.

He was partially educated at Walton RC School (the rest of his education happened over the next fifty years). He still clearly recalls one of his many motivational experiences at school, when he was told by the head teacher he *'would probably end up at the at the end of a rope'*. What a great sense of relief for him when they finally abolished hanging in 1964.

After leaving school he endured a five year apprenticeship in mechanical engineering before reluctantly agreeing with the HM Government to spend two years doing his National Service in the Army as a Military Bandsman in the 10th Royal Hussars.

His working life was spent in a variety of engineering jobs until boredom began to set in, and so he took up the challenge of semi retirement at 65, and then full retirement at 70.

John and his wife, Barbara now divide their time between visits to their daughter Julie and two grandchildren in California, and daughter Laura and the two grandchildren in Liverpool.

This book is based on original material researched for the two multi media DVDs John wrote and produced on Liverpool History.

All the proceeds from royalties raised are for the benefit of a local community-based charity which raises funds for homeless people in Liverpool, and a variety of Aid projects in the developing world.

Liverpool September 2007.

Introduction

This book is a combination of historic and contemporary data, mixed with some anecdotal material which I have gathered in the process of living in Liverpool for the last 70 years, and has subsequently been collected and processed during the last five years.

It describes the history of people and places, the events and dramas which gave to Liverpool, and to this book, the title of 'The Gateway to America'. The emphasis will always be on Maritime connections as they are the foundation for most of the connections to, and from, the United States.

My interest in Anglo-American connections, and more particularly those concerning Liverpool, began half way through World War Two.

As a five year old kid in Liverpool and attending Walton RC Infants School in the North end of the city, I came out of school one particular midday in November 1942 and was stopped in my tracks when I walked the small distance from the school to the main A59 Road at Walton Vale in North Liverpool.

A huge convoy of military vehicles and their U.S. Army drivers were making their way from Liverpool Docks to the newly established military base at Aintree Racecourse. For a small boy this certainly had enough of a wow factor to engage his undivided attention and from that point onwards I became aware that the wider world had arrived on my doorstep and the memory bank switched itself on.

Sixty years later in 2005 the BBC put up a web site to mark the sixtieth anniversary of the ending of World War Two entitled 'The Peoples War'. The BBC asked for memories and stories of the war years from a wide range of people to create a permanent record of the Second World War, but placing the emphasis firmly on the largely unrecorded views of us 'ordinary people'.

I thought I might contribute my memories about the arrival of the U.S. Army and the impact it had on the area where I live, and so began the process of research into the subject of Liverpool's American connections.

I began with the American military presence in Liverpool during World War Two.

Surprisingly, I could only find one visible link with that particular historic event. A six foot by two foot stone plaque which had been placed in the wall of the former floating roadway to the Landing Stage at the Pier Head. Over a period of time, I eventually found a considerable amount of data in various American archives. This led to me to produce a multi-media DVD on the subject and subsequently to the writing of this book.

The book is divided into four sections, and each section into chapters containing a variety of graphic images and information. It is designed to enable the reader to choose a particular area of interest by section or any particular chapter which is of interest to the reader.

Section One

Emigration

This section covers emigration from Liverpool to America. Initially the early links were exclusively one-way traffic from east to west and based on people from all over Britain, and later continental Europe, travelling to Liverpool, which was considered the shortest voyage, and also the least dangerous port of embarkation, to begin the long journey to the New World.

The emigration section has five subject chapters.

Pilgrims

In 1635 Richard Mather left his Liverpool Church at Toxteth and travelled to Massachusetts to eventually become one of the founders of Harvard College.

Penal Colonies

Most of us think of Australia when we read about convict transportation to the colonies, but before the American War of Independence, Britain sent large numbers of convicted persons, men, women and children to Virginia and to New England.

Irish Emigration

The largest ethnic group by far to emigrate from Liverpool was the huge wave of Irish people who went West to America during the famine years.

Mormon Emigration

Liverpool was chosen by the Mormon church leaders in Utah as the headquarters of their European missionary programme to recruit and convert people from northern Europe and transport them over 7000 miles to Salt Lake City.

Jewish Emigration

Liverpool became one of the principal ports of emigration for Jewish people from across Europe for a period of time in the nineteenth century. A small proportion of those settled here in Liverpool but the majority continued with their journey to the United States of America.

Section Two

Military Links

The American War of Independence

The links between Liverpool and the American Revolution were few in number but highly significant in their importance. The earliest military links of note began with the American Revolutionary War (1775 – 1783) or as the British establishment likes to call it 'The American War of Independence'.

Liverpool had its own regiment led by the son of the Lord Mayor which fought in the conflict known as '5th American Regiment' (British Legion), or 'The Liverpool Volunteers'.

There is an amazing true story of Liverpool born 'Mad Annie Bailey' who served as a scout and Indian fighter in the American Militia during the war of 1775.

And not forgetting Robert Morris (1734 – 1806) who was born in a small street off Dale Street, in the centre of Liverpool, and who emigrated to America as a young boy, he then went on to eventually become Treasurer to George Washington's new Government, and a signatory of the American Declaration of Independence.

The American Civil War

During the American Civil War of 1861 – 1865, Liverpool's powerful vested interests in the cotton trade ensured that it would side with the Confederate forces and many decisive events connected with the Civil War happened here – Captain James Dunwoody-Bulloch - principal representative of the Confederate Navy was sent to Liverpool to organise the building of warships. Liverpool became the 'de facto' European headquarters of the Confederate government, and played a role in the opening and closing phases of the conflict.

World War One

During the First World War (1914-1918), Liverpool was one the strategic ports of Britain's 'Western Approaches'.

When America finally entered the war against Germany on April 6th 1917, troops were sent to Europe almost immediately to join the Allies in France.

General Pershing landed at Liverpool with his US armies in June 1917. Liverpool became the first port of call for the American forces on their way to assist the British Army in achieving victory over Germany. As well as stores, weapons, and equipment which where shipped through the port in huge amounts, hundreds of thousands of US soldiers landed here and were placed in a huge transit camp built at Knotty Ash, on their way to the trenches in France.

World War Two

Liverpool was probably Britain's most important port during the second world war. It handled one third of the country's imports as it was the main terminus for Atlantic trade convoys. By early 1941 it had also become a major naval base and the headquarters of Britain's North Atlantic campaign.

An average of four convoys a week arrived from the USA in the Mersey during the war. Between 1939 and 1945 the port of Liverpool handled 75 million tons of cargo. Almost 74,000 airplanes and gliders were brought into the port. Over 4.7 million troops passed through en route to Normandy, of whom 1.2 million were American.

Section Three

Cultural Links

Liverpool's cultural links with America are probably stronger than anywhere else in the UK as would be expected, as it was for many centuries the main point of transatlantic travel from England to North America.

Entertainment

Present day American movie stars like Halle Berry, Kim Catterall, Mike Myers, Jeff and Beau Bridges all had one or more parents who were born in Liverpool and later emigrated to America.

Musical Links

The Beatles are the most obvious but there are many others.

Country and Western was big in Liverpool long before The Beatles and to a lesser degree Jazz artists like Louis Armstrong, Count Basie, Ella Fitzgerald.

Pop performers such as Bing Crosby, Frank Sinatra, Al Martino and many other American musicians and singing stars played in Liverpool throughout the fifties.

Literature

American authors such as Nathaniel Hawthorne, Herman Melville, Washington Irving, Mark Twain, had many strong links with Liverpool while British authors Felicia Hemans, Charles Dickens and Brian Jacques have strong Liverpool links with the USA.

Buildings and Institutions

It might be quicker to list the buildings that don't have an American connection, however here is a short list of the buildings that do have links.

Evered Avenue Library, in Rice Lane, Walton, was one of many libraries in Britain and throughout the USA, endowed by the Andrew Carnegie Trust.

Liverpool Cotton Exchange, which became the greatest market in the world for the buying and selling of cotton, particularly American cotton.

The Cunard Building, one of the famous 'three graces' at the Pier Head was the nerve centre of maritime traffic to North America.

Mersey Mission to Seamen in Liverpool, The Reverend James Fell was originally the Chaplain at the Mission in Hanover Street and later travelled to clean up the waterfront of San Francisco shortly after the Gold Rush.

William Brown Street Library, built by William Brown. Born in Northern Ireland, he emigrated to Baltimore becoming a rich merchant and came to Liverpool to represent his father's company. He built the famous Library for the City.

Liverpool University Art Gallery, John James Audubon was a nineteenth-century wildlife artist and naturalist. He travelled the American wilderness identifying, studying and drawing hundreds of species of birds and mammals.

The University holds the largest collection of original oil paintings by Audubon outside America.

Section Four

Trade and Commerce

Liverpool's trade with North America (USA & Canada) started in the 1660's (about 40 years before the slave trade began) bringing back tobacco and sugar.

As the continent developed, and ships became larger and faster, trade grew and Liverpool exported manufactured items such as cloth and pottery, and imported raw materials and foodstuffs'.

The Slave Trade

The Slave Trade triangle is a depressing piece of world history involving a variety of culprits in England, France, Spain, Portugal, African chiefs and traders, and the Arab countries of the Middle East. The victims were poor Africans - men, women, and children. Liverpool played a major role in the transportation of these poor victims of greed and exploitation, which constituted the second or middle part of the triangle of evil. An estimated 15 million Africans were transported as slaves to the Americas between 1540 and 1850.

Cotton Trade

Liverpool has been shaped by the many people and places involved in the cotton trade, particularly the southern states of the America. Liverpool is a cosmopolitan city and the global nature of the cotton trade helped contribute to this.

During the nineteenth century, American plantation owners in their top hats and frock coats, sold their produce in the open air on Exchange Flags behind Liverpool Town Hall.

Transatlantic Shipping

The Liverpool – American shipping links have inevitably evolved over many centuries and been driven by changing patterns of commerce, emigration and travel.

From the early 1700s ships sailing out of Liverpool began to increase slowly in numbers and were the prime source of historical linkage between Liverpool and North America, in fact without that shipping link, almost all of the other historical links would not have taken place.

Up until the 1960s the only practical way for passengers to cross the Atlantic was by ship, and one of the main UK departure ports was Liverpool. Two of the greatest Atlantic shipping lines, Cunard and White Star, were based in the city.

Since those maritime links have slowly declined down to the present container shipping link, the prospect of new linkages between Liverpool and the USA have now also ceased pro rata.

In the 21st century almost all trading from Liverpool to the USA now takes place from the giant container base at Seaforth Docks.

CHAPTER ONE

Emigration to America from Liverpool

Children of the Pilgrims

Emigration to the Americas began as early as 1585, but the first successful settlement was not established until Jamestown in 1607, with perhaps the most famous subsequent arrivals being that of the Mayflower from Plymouth in 1620 carrying a party of Puritans. Emigrants also went to work on the tobacco plantations in Virginia, many as indentured servants of the plantation owners.

The American settlements were also Britain's first penal colony, with many thousands of men, women and children from England, Scotland, Wales and Ireland sentenced to transportation in the 17th and 18th centuries. Although the sentences were usually only for 7 to 14 years, most would never be able to return home. Transportation to America ended with the American War of Independence in 1776.

Between 1830 and 1930 over 9 million emigrants sailed from Liverpool bound for a new life in the 'New World' countries such as the United States, Canada and Australia. For much of this period Liverpool was the most popular port of departure for emigrants from Europe to the Americas and Canada because she already had well established transatlantic links based on the import of cotton and timber.

Liverpool was also well placed to receive the many emigrants from the countries of north western Europe, who would cross the North Sea to Hull and then travel to Liverpool by train. Liverpool's share of the emigrant trade began to decline from the late 19th century as emigrants increasingly came from the countries of southern and eastern Europe.

There were three main motives for emigration.

Firstly, some of the emigrants were fleeing from the hardships of poverty and unemployment, for example, the 1.25 million Irish who emigrated between 1845 and 1851 as a result of the potato famine. For Russian and Polish Jews, emigration was a way of escaping from political and religious persecution. Other emigrants were not suffering the hardships of poverty or the terror of persecution, but were attracted by the possibility of a higher standard of living in the United States, Canada and elsewhere in the 'New World'.

The 'Gold Rush' in America also encouraged people to emigrate to make their fortunes. Emigrants could often spend from one to ten days or more, waiting for their ship in a Liverpool lodging house. In the late 1840s and 1850s, lodging houses were often inhospitable, dirty and overcrowded. In the mid-19th century emigrants passing through Liverpool were also subject to harassment and fraud by local confidence tricksters, known as 'runners' who would frequently snatch emigrants' luggage and would only return it on payment of a large fee.

From the 1860s the situation began to improve as steam started to replace sail on the Atlantic route. The steamship companies started to look after the emigrants during their stay in Liverpool with their representatives meeting them on arrival in Liverpool, and taking them to lodging houses which were often owned by the steamship companies.

Until the early 1860s most emigrants left Liverpool on a sailing ship. The voyage to the United States and Canada took about 35 days. Emigrating in a sailing ship could be unpleasant, particularly during a storm.

Seasickness was a particular problem on the stormy North Atlantic westbound voyage, and diseases such as cholera and typhus frequently reached epidemic proportions as infection spread throughout the confined decks.

By 1870 virtually all emigrants to the United States and Canada went by steamship and the voyage was consequently reduced to between seven and ten days.

An Early Emigrant from Liverpool

Revd. Richard Mather

Richard Mather, Minister of Toxteth Chapel, Park Road, Dingle, Liverpool. Born 1596 at Lowton, Warrington, Lancashire. Died April 22nd 1669, Dorchester, Massachusetts.

Richard Mather, matriculated at Brasenose College, Oxford in 1618, but studied there for only a few months.

After he began preaching at Toxteth Park Chapel in Liverpool late in 1633, the Church of England decided to remove him from the pulpit. His offences are not known, although they were doubtless ecclesiastical; he did not conform to the practices of the Church of England in many ways.

He and his family then emigrated to the British colony at Massachusetts Bay, arriving in mid-August 1635.

In Dorchester, Massachusetts the townsfolk had been unable to organise their church in April 1636. They were however successful in the August of that year and Richard Mather was immediately inaugurated as church leader. He served the church and community quietly and faithfully for many years.

Although in most ways he resembled a typical Puritan minister of that time in Massachusetts Bay Colony, in several notable accomplishments he differed.

He published a defence of the 'New England Way' as the church policy of the

Toxteth Chapel, Park Road, Liverpool 2007

Bay Colony was called; and he helped to write the Cambridge Platform (1648) defining ecclesiastical policy; he also contributed to the definition of Puritan baptismal practice in the so-called Halfway Covenant (1662); and served as an overseer of Harvard College.

Richard Mather was to all intents the earliest known notable person, to make the transition from Liverpool to America.

Members of three successive generations of the Mather family were Puritan ministers in the Massachusetts Bay Colony in New England: Richard (1596–1669), Increase (1629–1723), and Cotton (1663–1728).

Each achieved fame as a preacher and writer, and collectively they exerted a formative influence on the religious life of colonial America.

CHAPTER THREE

British Penal Colonies in North America

America was Britain's first penal colony, with many thousands of men, women and children from England, Scotland, Wales and Ireland sentenced to transportation in the 17th and 18th centuries. Although the sentences were usually only for 7 to 14 years, most would never be able to return home.

Some political offenders in the eighteenth century were, no doubt, sold into a longer or shorter American servitude.

The Gentleman's Magazine stated, on May 31, 1747, that *'430 rebel prisoners from the jails of Lancaster, Carlisle, Chester, York, and Lincoln were transported this month from Liverpool to the American Plantations.*

Eight of them were drowned by a boat over-setting, not being able to swim because they were handcuffed.

This number, with the rest, makes above a thousand rebels transported'.

The first occurrence of child emigration from England was during the early 17th century, when the London Common Council sent out 100 vagrant children to the first permanent English settlement in North America, Jamestown in Virginia in 1619.

More vagrant and poor children were sent out following the Privy Council's authorisation of child migration in 1620 with, for example, a 100 vagrant children being sent out amongst the reinforcements following the Indian Massacre of the settlers in Virginia in 1622.

The British used North America as a penal colony through the system of indentured servants. Most notably, the Province of Georgia was originally designed as a penal colony. Convicts would be transported by private sector merchants and auctioned off to plantation owners upon arrival in the colonies.

> *'All this is a rehash of all the emigration schemes, voluntary or coerced, as a form of hope or as a form of punishment — both leading to redemption, I am sure, in Protestant thinking — which began in Liverpool in 1648 when the mayor made a contract with local ship owners to rid the city streets of its orphaned childbeggars by transplanting them to the American colonies.'*

Professor François Poirier – University of Paris

It is estimated that some 60,000 British convicts were banished to colonial America, representing perhaps one-quarter of all British emigrants during the eighteenth century.

Transportation to America ended with the American War of Independence in 1776. It was not however to be the end of convict transportation as the Crown authorities switched their penal colonies to the more expensive and difficult location of Australia.

CHAPTER FOUR

Irish Emigration

Early image of an Irish family eviction. For the dispossessed there were only two alternatives – begging or emigration

A rapidly increasing population in Ireland at the end of the 18th century led to the exploitation of land and the increasing of rents followed by forced evictions by the landlords. This was exacerbated by the disastrous famine of 1847 and led to an exodus of biblical proportions to England, and for the most part, via Liverpool, on to America.

What follows are extracts from an article printed in the **Illustrated London News** on Saturday, July 6th, 1850. It is a contemporary account of the procedure of Emigration from the port of Liverpool to the New World and the Colonies.

'The annals of the modern world offer no such record as that presented in the history of Ireland, since the memorable and deplorable years of the potato famine, and of the pestilence that followed in its track. The splendid emigrant ships that ply between Liverpool and New York, and which have sufficed in previous years to carry to the shores of America an Irish emigration, amounting on the average to 250,000 souls per annum, have, during the present spring, been found insufficient to transport to the States the increasing swarms of Irish who have resolved to try in the New World to gain the independence which has been denied them in the old'.

Once they made the decision to emigrate to America, the preparation was very complex, and represented for the emigrants a detailed exercise of travel planning. The usual road taken by the emigrants bound to America ended in Dublin. From there the emigrant crossed to Liverpool, and took a ship sailing to New York, Boston or Philadelphia.

Departure of the 'Nimrod' and 'Athlone' steamers with emigrants on board, for Liverpool.

The following extract comes from a contemporary English newspaper report.

'The great tide of Emigration flows steadily westward. The principal emigrants are Irish peasants and labourers. It is calculated that at least four out of every five persons who leave the shores of the old country to try their fortunes in the new, are Irish. Since the fatal years of the potato famine and the cholera, the annual numbers of emigrants have gone on increasing, until they have become so great as to suggest the idea, and almost justify the belief, of a gradual depopulation of Ireland.

The colonies of Great Britain offer powerful attractions to the great bulk of the English and Scottish emigrants who forsake their native land to make homes in the wilderness.

But the Irish emigration flows with full force upon the United States. Though many of the Irish emigrants are, doubtless, persons of small means, who have been hoarding and saving for years, and living in rags and squalor, in order to amass sufficient money to carry themselves and families across the Atlantic, and to beg their way to the western states.

There they may 'squat' or purchase cheap lands, the great bulk appears to be people of the most destitute class, who go to join their friends and relatives, previously established in America.

Large sums of money reach this country annually from the United States. Through Liverpool houses alone, near upon a million pounds sterling, in small drafts, varying from two pounds or three pounds to ten pounds each, are annually forwarded from America, for poor persons in Ireland, to enable them to emigrate; and the passage-money of many thousands, in addition, is paid in New York. Before the fatal year 1847, the emigration was very considerable; but, since that time, it has very rapidly increased.

The walls of Liverpool are thoroughly placarded with the notices of the days of sailing of the various packets, for which many firms act as passenger-brokers, and set forth in large letters the excellent qualities of such well known and favourite packets as the 'Yorkshire', the 'New World', the 'Isaac Webb', the 'West Point', the 'Constitution', the 'Isaac Wright', the 'London', the 'Star of the West', the 'Queen of the West', and scores of others.

The average number of steerage passengers that can be accommodated in these fine vessels (which are mostly owned in New York) is 400; but some of them, such as the 'Isaac Webb', can comfortably make room for double that number.

After the emigrant has chosen the ship by which he will sail, and perhaps run the gauntlet through scores of designing and unscrupulous 'man-catchers'-a class of persons who get a commission from the passenger-brokers for each emigrant that they bring to the office-his next duty is to present himself at the Medical Inspector's Office.

The scene in the Waterloo dock, at Liverpool, where all the American sailing packets are stationed, is at all times a very busy one; but, on the morning of the departure of a large ship, with a full complement of emigrants, it is peculiarly exciting and interesting. The scenes that occur between decks on the day before the sailing of a packet, and during the time that a ship may be unavoidably detained in dock, are not generally of a character to impress the spectator with the idea of any great or overwhelming grief on the part of the emigrants at leaving the old country.

On the contrary, all is bustle, excitement, and merriment. The scene of a party of emigrants, male and female, dancing between decks-to the music of the violin-played for their amusement, by some of their fellow-passengers, is not a rare one.

But, as the hour of departure draws nigh, the music ceases. Too many fresh arrivals take place every moment, and the docks become too much encumbered with luggage to admit of the amusement. Although notice of the day and hour of departure may have been given for weeks previously, there are a large class of persons (not confined to emigrants it may be observed 'en passant') who never will be punctual, and who seem to make it a point of duty and conscience to postpone everything to the last moment.

There are usually a large number of spectators at the dock-gates to witness the final departure of the noble ship, with its large freight of human beings. It is an interesting and impressive sight; and the most callous and indifferent can scarcely fail, at such a moment, to form cordial wishes for the pleasant voyage and safe arrival of the emigrants, and for their future prosperity in their new home.

As the ship is towed out, hats are raised, handkerchiefs are waved, and a loud and long-continued shout of farewell is raised from the shore, and cordially responded to from the ship. It is then, if at any time, that the eyes of the emigrants begin to moisten with regret at the thought that they are looking for the last time at the old country-that country which, although, in all probability, associated principally with the remembrance of sorrow and suffering, of semi-starvation, and a constant battle for the merest crust necessary to support existence.

Immigrants arriving in New York

The ship has to pay a poll-tax of one dollar and a half per passenger to the State of New York; and if any of the poor emigrants are helpless and deformed persons, the owners are fined in the sum of 75 dollars for bringing them, and are compelled to enter a bond to the city of New York that they will not become a burden on the public. To prevent this risk, the medical officer of the ship passes them under inspection; and if there be a pauper cripple among the number who cannot give security that he has friends in America to take charge of him of arrival, and provide for him afterwards, the captain may refuse to take him.

The business of verification and inspection generally occupies from two to four hours, according to the number of emigrants on board; and, during its progress, some noteworthy incidents occasionally arise.

Sometimes an Irishman, with a wife and eight or ten children, who may have only paid a deposit of his passage-money, attempts to evade the payment of the balance, by pleading that he has not a farthing left in the world; and trusting that the ship will rather take him out to New York for the sum already paid, than incur the trouble of putting him on shore again with his family.

Sometimes a woman may have included in her passage-ticket an infant at the breast, and may be seen, when her name is called, panting under the weight of a boy of eight or nine years of age, whom she is holding to her bosom as if he were really a suckling.

Sometimes a youth of 19 strong and big as a man, has been entered as under

12 in order to get across to America for half the fare of an adult; and sometimes a whole family are without any tickets, and have come on board in the hope that, amid the confusion which they imagine will be attendant upon the congregation of so many hundred people on a ship, they may manage to evade notice, and slip down unperceived amid those whose documents are found .

Those who have money, and have attempted a fraud, generally contrive, after many lamentations about their extreme poverty, to produce the necessary funds, which, in the shape of golden sovereigns are not infrequently found to be safely stitched amid the rags of petticoats, coats, and unmentionable garments.

Those who have really no money, and who cannot manage to appeal to the sympathy of the crowd for a small subscription to help them to the New World, must resign themselves to their fate, and remain in the poverty from which they seek to free themselves, until they are able to raise the small sum necessary for their emancipation.

The stowaways, if any, are ordered to be taken before the magistrates; and all strangers and interlopers being safely placed in the tug, the emigrant ship is left to herself.

May all prosperity attend her and her living freight!'

There are some 40 million Irish Americans in the United States of America, the descendants of those who sailed from Liverpool over the past four centuries, crossing the Atlantic in successive waves of emigrations.

Life in America was very rarely easy and many of the new immigrants fell by the wayside; but eventually they achieved a standard of living unimaginable in the world they had left behind.

John F. Kennedy

Over the generations they rose to the highest positions in politics, the labour movement, the professions, industry, commerce and the arts, and their very numbers made them a powerful political force.

The election of John F. Kennedy as President of the United States epitomises the progress of Irish emigration to America. Of Irish descent, he was born in Brookline, Massachusetts, on May 29, 1917, the great grandson of one of the first wave of Irish immigrants to arrive in Boston.

In 1961 millions watched his television debates with the Republican candidate, Richard M. Nixon.

Winning by a narrow margin in the popular vote, Kennedy became the first Catholic President of the United States of America.

Tragically, he was assassinated on November 22, 1963, in Dallas, Texas.

James (Big Jim) Larkin (Irish: Séamas Ó Lorcáin) 21 January 1876 - 30 January 1947, an Irish trade union leader and socialist activist, was born in Liverpool, England in 1876, of Irish parents although he and his family later moved to live in a small cottage in Burren, in South Down.

Growing up in poverty, he had little formal education and began working in a variety of jobs while still a child before becoming a full-time trade union organiser in 1905.

He moved to Ireland in 1907, where he founded the Irish Transport and General Workers' Union, the Irish Labour Party, and later the Workers' Union of Ireland.

Larkin's family lived in the slums in Liverpool during the early years of his life, and from the age of seven he attended school in the mornings and worked in the afternoons to supplement the family income - a common arrangement in working-class families at the time.

At the age of fourteen, after the death of his father, he was apprenticed to the Liverpool engineering firm his father had worked for, but was dismissed after two years.

He was unemployed for a while and then worked as a seaman and docker.

By 1903 he was a dock foreman, and on 8 September that year he married Elizabeth Brown.

From 1893 Larkin had developed an interest in socialism, and he became a member of the Independent Labour Party.

In 1905 he was one of the few foremen to take part in a strike on the Liverpool docks.

He was elected to the strike committee, and although he lost his foreman's job as a result, his performance had so impressed the National Dock Labourers' Union (NDLU) that it appointed him a temporary organiser.

Larkin in America, 1914–1923

Some months after the lockout ended, Larkin left for the United States. He intended to recuperate from the strain of the lockout and raise funds for the union. His decision to leave dismayed many union activists. Once there he became a member of the Socialist Party of America, and was involved in the Industrial Workers of the World union.

He became an enthusiastic supporter of the Soviet Union and was expelled from the Socialist Party of America in 1919 along with numerous other sympathisers of the Bolsheviks.

Larkin's speeches in support of the Soviet Union, his association with founding members of the American Communist Party, and his radical publications made him a target of the 'Red Scare' that was sweeping the nation.

The support by radicals for the Russian Revolution worried Woodrow Wilson and his administration and America entered what became known as the 'Red Scare' period. On 7th November 1919, the second anniversary of the revolution, Alexander Mitchell Palmer, Wilson's attorney general, ordered the arrest of over 10,000 suspected communists and anarchists.

This included Larkin who was charged with 'advocating force, violence and unlawful means to overthrow the Government'.

Larkin's trial began on 30th January 1920. He decided to defend himself. He denied that he had advocated the overthrow of the Government.

However, he admitted that he was part of the long American revolutionary tradition that included Abraham Lincoln, Walt Whitman, Henry David Thoreau and Ralph Waldo Emerson. He also quoted Wendell Phillips in his defence: 'Government exists to protect the rights of minorities. The loved and the rich need no protection – the rich have many friends and the loved few enemies.'

The jury found Larkin guilty of 'criminal anarchy' and on 3rd May 1920 he received a sentence of between five to ten years in Sing Sing.

In prison Larkin worked in the bootery, manufacturing and repairing shoes.

In November 1922, Alfred Smith won the election for Governor in New York. A few days later he ordered an investigation of the imprisonment of Larkin and on 17th January 1923 he granted him a free pardon and deported him back to Ireland.

Jim Larkin returned home to a triumphant reception.

Sing Sing Prison

Soon after Larkin established a new union, the Workers' Union of Ireland (WUI). He also became head of the Irish section of the Comintern and visited the Soviet Union in 1924 and 1928.

Larkin successfully built up the WUI and in February 1932 won the North Dublin seat in the Dail. However, he lost the seat in January 1933. Larkin was also forced to close down 'The Irish Worker'. Later he started another radical newspaper, 'Irish Workers' Voice'.

In the next election he won the North-East Dublin seat. However, in 1944 he was once again defeated at the polls.

The following year his application to join the Irish Labour Party was finally accepted. James Larkin died in his sleep on 30th January, 1947, aged 71 years.

Today a statue of 'Big Jim' stands on O'Connell Street in Dublin. The inscription on the front of the monument is an extract from one of his famous speeches:

'The great appear great because we are on our knees:
Let us rise.'

CHAPTER FIVE

Mormon Emigration

Apart from a bronze statue erected at the Pier Head in 2003 by the Mormon Church in America, very little evidence of that period of Liverpool's history features visibly as a contemporary historical asset of the city.

This chapter of the book attempts to restore the balance in the interests of historical accuracy.

Liverpool was the European H.Q. for the transportation of Mormon emigrants to the United States up to 1868, and was described at that time as 'The Springboard to Zion - Utah, USA'.

Of 333 ships chartered to sail to US East coast ports, 209 began their journey in Liverpool, between 1840 and 1890.

During the period 1847-1853, at least 59 emigrant ships sank during their Atlantic crossing.

The journey from England to America was sometimes referred to as 'the Mormon Trail', it stretched all the way from Liverpool to Salt Lake City, making it by far the longest of any trail west.

The importance of Liverpool in the history of Mormon emigration from Europe, and a valuable insight into life and conditions in the port during the nineteenth century, is graphically described in the book 'Saints on the Seas' by Conway B. Sonne.

The ship Ellen Maria pictured leaving Liverpool in 1853,
carrying Mormon converts on the first leg of their epic journey to Utah.
Painting by Ken Baxter – ©LDS (Mormon Church).

'No seaport was more important in the Mormon migration than Liverpool

Since the great majority of emigrants came from the United Kingdom and the European continent, this vibrant city was the principal staging area for their Atlantic crossing.

Of the 333 identified voyages of Mormon emigrant companies through 1890, Liverpool was the port of embarkation for 289. Liverpool had many natural advantages.

It was centrally located between Great Britain and Ireland. It was quite accessible by rail from London and the eastern ports of England, such as Hull and Grimsby.

The harbour had easily navigable channels, being situated just a few miles up the Mersey Estuary from the Irish Sea and Liverpool Bay.

Liverpool was also a day's sail nearer in distance to America and, because of the delays in moving up and down the English Channel and River Thames, several days nearer in time than London.

Arriving at Liverpool, the Mormon convert found a crescent shaped harbour thriving on marine traffic.'

Upwards of 20,000 vessels entered and left the River Mersey each year. Liverpool grew up on the east bank of the estuary opposite Birkenhead on the west bank.

The traveller would see a forest of masts, for the harbour was filled with craft of every description.

There were sleek clipper ships, square-rigged packets from America, schooners, barks, brigs, snows, sloops, steamers, tugs, and fishing boats—all crowded in and around the docks anchored in the Mersey, or moving in or out of the estuary.

Colourful pennants and flags of many nations flew in the breeze, and the docks were lined with ornamented bows and figureheads.

The nineteenth century was Liverpool's golden age. In the previous century the city had become the hub of the notorious Liverpool Triangle.

This term was applied to a three-cornered trade. Ships sailing out of Liverpool carried trinkets and cheap cotton goods to West Africa in exchange for black slaves.

These slaves were transported to the West Indies and sold for cargoes of sugar, cotton, and other raw materials.

Early in the nineteenth century this triangular trade ceased, and Liverpool was revitalized by the flowering industrial revolution and the phenomenon of westward emigration.

Once again Liverpool became a port bursting with activity. By 1840 its population had grown to over 200,000.

The focal point of commercial life was the Pier Head, which was adjacent to the floating landing stage used to disembark passengers from ships of all flags.

Liverpool was well on the way toward constructing some of the finest dock facilities in the world.

These docks formed a belt along the waterfront and were given such names as Prince's, Victoria, Waterloo, George's, Albert, and King's.

There were basically three kinds of docks: wet docks which retained water through a system of gates, permitting large ships to float up to the pier, dry docks which became dry as the tide receded, and graving docks in which the water could be controlled to facilitate the repair of ships.

Incoming vessels were not always able to find dock space or had to anchor offshore until the tide changed.

Brigham Young recorded upon his arrival at Liverpool on April 6, 1840, *'We landed in Liverpool; I got into a boat with Elders Kimball and P.P. Pratt, and when I landed on the shore I gave a loud shout of thanksgiving.*

We procured a room at No. 8, Union Street. The ship failing to get into the dock with the tide, I sent a boat for brothers O. Pratt, Geo. A. Smith and R. Hedlock.'

Liverpool was expanding its docks, warehouses, and sheds along the water's edge but the city itself was also being built up.

Along the dock area were rows of artisans' houses, and over the years a Custom House, St. Georges' Hall, Victoria Tower, a Town Hall, Lyceum, and railroad station on Lime Street would be built. The city was a mixture of old and new.

Its grey drabness belied the energy and verve of its people, increased considerably by an inflow of Irish workers.

Its streets were alive with American, English, African, Asian, and other foreign seamen seeking their diversions from pubs, panderers, and prostitutes.

One visitor said, *'In Liverpool decent chaps owned ships, fairly decent chaps brokered cotton, almost decent chaps brokered corn—the rest just didn't exist.'*

A rival of London, Liverpool was a city of almost everything—yet all things were not favourable.

Tides in the harbour could range up to twenty-nine feet. Winters were often severe, although ice seldom caused navigational problems in the Mersey. Winds were frequently contrary.

Since these winds during the winter months could reach gale force from the west and northwest, sailing packets sometimes delayed their scheduled departures for several days.

Eventually tugs were used to tow the ships out of the estuary.

Delays could also be caused by the frequent fogs which blanketed the harbour and city.

Despite these drawbacks, mariners regarded Liverpool as one of the finest ports in the world.

The Mormon emigrant saw in Liverpool a city of contrasts. The rich and poor were worlds apart.

It was a haven of churches but a home of brothels. It was overcrowded, rambunctious, and tough.

For all of its virtues and vices, Liverpool had a cosmopolitan excitement; and the Mormon convert experienced mingled hope and anxiety in his strange surroundings.

To him Liverpool was the place of the first gathering, the springboard to Zion.

In keeping with the flight of the fabulous bird Liver, from which its name was supposedly derived, from 1840 on this great port winged its way solidly into Mormon history.

For more than a decade the Mormon emigration consisted entirely of British converts, and with the exception of two sailings from Bristol these Saints gathered at and later sailed from Liverpool.

Later in the book, on page 51, he describes the vessels and crews which were used to cross the Atlantic at that time.

'Although many transient sailing vessels carried Mormon emigrants to America, packet ships accounted for a significant number of Atlantic passages under canvas. In the mid-nineteenth century there were fifty sailing packet lines in transatlantic service from Liverpool. Of these lines thirty-six ran to New York, five to Philadelphia, four to New Orleans, three to Boston, one to Baltimore, and one to Charleston.

Such packet lines were served by the most skilled, rugged, and hard-bitten seamen afloat.

Packets lived for speed. To meet a timetable – with almost fanatical determination – their officers and crews challenged the wild Atlantic on their own terms. In summer and winter, night and day, fair weather and foul these strong and sturdy square-riggers maximized canvas – often carrying sail when it was impossible for sailors to go aloft to take it in. In a word, packets were built to fight the seas.

Their masters were expected to fight time, to keep a schedule. In fact, the stress was so great that the average packet captain was burned out after about five years in the transatlantic trade.

Their bucko mates were trained to fight and drive reluctant crews with fists and belaying pins.

These tough, hard, and frequently brutal officers believed they had to prove themselves a match for their disreputable crews, known as 'packet rats,' too often supplied by New York and Liverpool crimps through trickery, drugs, and alcohol.

These wooden ships were sailed by men of steel, hardened by the world's hardest school of seamanship'.

John Taylor, born in Liverpool in 1808, was converted to Mormonism in

John Taylor

Canada, and quickly became a key leader, active in organizing the astonishingly successful Mormon mission to Great Britain.

He was present at all the crises of Mormonism: the financial ruin in Kirtland, Ohio; the ugly expulsion from Missouri; the mob murder of Joseph Smith (Taylor took four musket balls in his own body trying to protect his prophet); the exodus west; the coming of the federal army to Utah; and the death of Brigham Young.

More than that, he was an intellectual, an able editor, as well as a missionary organizer, and was respected by Brigham Young as 'a mighty man'. Elder John Taylor was the first Mormon missionary to preach in Liverpool. He arrived on 11 January 1840.

He first preached in churches or buildings as offered to him, but soon determined to hire the Music Hall on Bold Street for his own series of lectures and for Church services after a branch was established.

Following Elder Taylor's return to the United States, the hall continued to be used by the Mormon Church for meetings and conferences. A gala farewell for Brigham Young returning to the United States was held here in April 1841.

John Taylor was with Joseph and Hyrum Smith in Carthage Jail, Illinois, awaiting a court hearing regarding the destruction of an anti-Mormon newspaper, when the Smith brothers were killed by an angry mob.

John Taylor tried to escape out of a window and was shot five times, he managed to evade his pursuers and became known as a 'living martyr', later becoming the Church's third President.

In succeeding years when the headquarters of the Church was in Liverpool, the Music Hall served as the site for mission conferences and large meetings.

The great hall where Church services and Elder Taylor's lectures were held is one floor above ground level.

Today the Music Hall is a Wine Bar and is situated right in the heart of Liverpool's clubland.

The Music Hall in Bold Street

It is on the corner of Concert Street and Bold Street, occupying several floors.

Before that period, the Mormon Hall was situated at 15 Wilton Street, Liverpool during the years up to 1857, then it was relocated to 42 Islington.

Information taken from the archives of Pioneer History Museum In Salt Lake City, Utah.

An account by a group of Danish Mormons traveling to Utah in 1873

'It was wonderful to see so many ships in the English Channel. In Hull we were but three hours. We went the same evening by train to Liverpool. I think Hull is about the size of Copenhagen. It was bad we went through England in the night, as we passed many trains and cities and through tunnels and over rivers and lakes. We rode the 44 miles in seven hours and

arrived in Liverpool at 8 a.m. on the 19th of January.

Here we got beds; the first we have had since we left Copenhagen. We have had to lay on straw, on boards and boxes, and have had many trials.

There is no end to see in Liverpool. It has 500,000 inhabitants and is several miles in circumference. It has many large stores and factories and buildings not equalled in Denmark but the most wonderful is the shipping. I think there are 100 harbours and 1000 ships in each.

I cannot describe all there is to see great butcher shops, beef seven cents, pork six cents. We do not see rye bread at all but wheat bread everywhere. They mix oat and cornmeal together.

We lay in Liverpool 15 days before setting sail for New York'.

The Mormon European headquarters at Islington in Liverpool was the place where the journey began.

Everything for the journey to Utah was bought here, the payment for the transatlantic ship journey, provisions, and even payment of £75 for four Oxen and the special wagons,

Mormon European Headquarters, Islington, Liverpool 1890

known as the Connestoga Wagon for the 1300 mile trek across the plains from Nauvoo, Illinois through Iowa, Nebraska, Wyoming to the Rocky Mountains and eventually, to Salt Lake City, Utah.

Connestoga Wagon, or 'Prairie Schooner' as it was sometimes called, was one of the main vehicles used to transport people, and all they would need to begin a new life in the wilderness of the American West.

The trail was not a narrow path, but a corridor, depending on the river, on available grass, on the terrain, events of the year and other factors.

The Connestoga Wagon

The motivations for moving west were unique. The Mormons did not travel west for gold, land or adventure.

They went west in search of religious freedom and to maintain a cultural identity. Mormon wagon companies were highly organized and disciplined units, if they had not been, they would not have survived the the difficulties and hardships that lay ahead.

They were often required to cross deep wide rivers on their long journey, some of the ferries they built helped finance the movement.

They planted crops; they recorded pertinent information such as the topography, latitude, longitude, distances, flora and fauna.

The Mormon Trail is 1,032 miles from Winter Quarters (Nebraska) to Salt Lake City,Utah.

The Mormon Trail was used for 23 years, from 1846 to 1869.

In 1856, the church inaugurated a system of handcart companies in order to enable poor European emigrants to make the trek more cheaply.

The emigrants would carry their goods and provisions on small handcarts, which they pushed or pulled along the trail.

Handcarts were used from 1856-1860. Nearly 3,000 migrants used this method of transportation.

They could make 25-30 miles a day (a wagon would travel 10-15 miles a day). There were ten handcart companies.

Five companies made the trek in 1856, and the last two – the Willie and Martin Handcart Companies met disaster when they left very late and encountered heavy snow and freezing weather in Wyoming. This could sometimes mean whole wagon trains, men, women children and animals, freezing to death.

Brigham Young organized a rescue effort that brought the companies in, but more than 210 of the 980 emigrants in the two parties died.

Everyone was expected to follow their leader and to obey the rules.

They had a daily routine. There was discipline, hard work, mutual assistance and devotional practices. As a rule they did not travel on Sunday.

Knowing that others would follow, pioneers improved the trail and built support facilities.

The handcart companies continued with more success until 1860, and traditional ox-and-wagon companies also continued for those who could afford the higher cost.

After 1860 the church began sending wagon companies east each spring, to return to Utah in the summer with the emigrating Latter-day Saints.

As the Mormons were preparing to go west, they were approached by the United States government for help in the war against Mexico.

The Mormon Battalion was formed with over 500 members near Council Bluffs, Iowa in 1846.

They then began a march to San Diego, California, one of the longest marches in military history.

They never fought a battle, but made history by clearing roads to the west and helping to secure California as a U.S. Territory.

Some former members eventually participated in the discovery of gold at Sutter's Mill.

Finally, with the completion of the Transcontinental Railroad in 1869, future emigrants were able to travel by rail, and the era of the Mormon pioneer trail came to an end.

Salt Lake City, Utah

Salt Lake City is now the headquarters of The Church of Jesus Christ of Latterday Saints (the LDS. or Mormon Church).

The city was founded in 1847 by a group of Mormon pioneers led by their prophet, Brigham Young, who fled hostility from the mid west.

Today, Salt Lake City is the capital and the most populous city in the U.S. State of Utah.

Mining booms and the construction of the first transcontinental railroad initially brought economic growth, and the city became nicknamed the Crossroads of the West.

In the 21st century Salt Lake City has developed a strong outdoor recreation industry, and has become the industrial banking centre of the U.S.

The City served as host to the 2002 Winter Olympics.

CHAPTER SIX

Jewish Emigration from Liverpool

Jewish emigrants waiting to board

In 1882 an extensive programme of emigration to America was organized and directed from Liverpool; and during the year of the Russo-Jewish persecutions 6,274 persons were sent, at a cost of over £30,000 ($150,000), to the United States and Canada in steamships from the Port of Liverpool. The ports of Le Havre, Antwerp, Rotterdam, Genoa and especially Liverpool were all important ports of emigration.

Arnold Lewis, Chairman of the Liverpool Jewish Historical Society

'The Jewish community goes much further back than the beginning of the 1900's, there is a misconception that the Jewish people only arrived in Liverpool round about 1900 when there were Pogroms in Russia and Poland and thousands of them decided to emigrate to America.

That's when the majority of Jewish families settled in Liverpool, they had to go through the UK and the boats brought them over, they came through by train to Liverpool with the plan to get on the boat to America and although a lot of them actually did go to America, hundreds of them decided to stay in Liverpool.

Because they arrived by train, immediately behind Lime Street Station was the neighbourhood where they decide to settle, in the Brownlow Hill, Copperas Hill, Pembroke Place and the Crown Street area.

We interviewed one man who remembers when the trans-migrants came from Russia ready to go, they weren't staying in Liverpool so they were put up in lodgings over night near the Oceanic Hotel and places like that by the shipping companies while they had to wait for the ship going off to the States.'

He recalls going down there when he was a young child, and they would come and do street entertainments while they were waiting for the ship to take them to America, they would play the accordions which they managed to bring with them, and he used to delight in it and remembers very clearly the atmosphere that they produced during the very little time they spent in Liverpool, just in the two or three days before they were shipped on elsewhere.'

Russian Jewish emigrants board the SS Thetis at Liverpool Landing Stage

CHAPTER SEVEN

American Military Links

Robert Morris

American Revolution – 1775.

Y ou may be surprised at the number of historical military links that exist between Liverpool and America, and not just from World War Two.

Robert Morris was born on January 31, 1734 in Dale Street, Liverpool, the son of a nail maker who emigrated to Oxford, Maryland which was a busy port on Chesapeake Bay and served as an agent for a Liverpool tobacco merchant. Young Robert displayed an aptitude for business and was apprenticed with merchant Charles Willing.

By 1754, he was a partner and the firm grew to be one of the largest merchant firms in Philadelphia, with its own fleet of ships which sailed to Europe and the West Indies.

A signatory of The Declaration of Independence and Articles of Confederation, Superintendent of Finance, 1781-84, he established The Bank of North America and became a United States Senator, 1789-95.

Morris's portrait appeared on US $1000 notes from 1862 to 1863 and on the $10 silver certificates from 1878 to 1880, along with Alexander Hamilton and Albert Gallatin.

Morris is considered one of the key founders of the financial system in the United States. Morris and Roger Sherman were the only two people to sign the three significant founding documents of the United States, the Declaration of Independence, the Articles of Confederation, and the U.S. Constitution.

In the language of an elegant historian of the American war, **Rev. Charles A. Goodrich** - Lives of the Signers to the Declaration of Independence. New York: William Reed & Co., 1856. *'Certainly the Americans owed and still owe, as much acknowledgment to the financial operations of Robert Morris, as to the negotiations of Benjamin Franklin, or even the arms of George Washington.'*

'He provided the funds which enabled General Washington to move his army towards the south, and which led to the decisive battle which terminated the war. It may be truly said, so we may have some idea of the nature and magnitude of the services rendered by Mr. Morris to the United States.

That few men acted a more conspicuous or useful part; and when we recollect, that it was by his exertions and talents, that the United States were so often relieved from their difficulties, at times of great depression and pecuniary distress, an estimate may be formed of the weight of obligations due to him from the people of the present day.

It may be proper to add, however, that the latter part of his life was rendered unhappy, by an unfortunate scheme of land speculation, in which he engaged, and by which his pecuniary affairs became exceedingly embarrassed; yet amidst his severest trials, he maintained a firmness and an independence of character, which in similar circumstances belong to but few.

At length, through public labour, and private misfortune, his constitution was literally worn out, and like a shock of corn fully ripe, Robert Morris came to his end on the 4th of May, 1806, in the 72nd year of his age'.

CHAPTER EIGHT

Mad Annie Bailey

Annie Trotter Bailey

The story of 'Mad Annie' is probably the most incredible and bizarre story concerning Liverpool connections with America – and the least known about – particularly in Britain.

Annie Trotter Bailey was born in Liverpool, England as Anne Hennis in 1742. She went to live with relatives when her parents died in 1761. Her relatives lived in Virginia near Staunton in the Shenandoah Valley, U.S.A. She married Richard Trotter in 1765 and had one son named William. Richard was killed in a battle on October 19, 1774. After he died, Annie left William with a neighbour named Mrs. Moses Mann. Then Annie dressed herself like a man and joined the army. She went to many militia meetings to tell the men to fight the British or the Indians.

This event changed Annie's life completely and so she became a skilled frontier scout, horsewoman, hunter, messenger and storyteller, wearing buckskins, carrying hatchet, knife and long rifle. 'Mad Annie' and her black horse named 'Liverpool', carried out many dangerous and daring missions during the Indian Wars.

Many fanciful stories have been told about Annie, some perhaps of her own origin. Henry Howe missed Annie's story when he wrote his first history of Ohio in the 1840's, but soon learned it in West Virginia. Mr. Howe recounts it thus:

'On one occasion, when she was pursued by Indians, she came to an impenetrable thicket

where she was obliged to dismount and leave him [her fine black horse, Liverpool] *for their capture.*

She then crawled into a hollow sycamore log. The Indians came and rested on the log, but without suspecting her trick.

After they had gone she followed their trail, and in the darkness of night recaptured the animal, and, mounting him, when at a safe distance from being shot or taken, gave a shout of defiance and bounded away.'

She married again in 1785 to John Bailey, another frontiersman and army ranger.

They moved to Clendenin's Settlement in the Great Kanawha Valley where she would make her famous ride. The story of Annie Bailey's life is interwoven with local folklore, but her place as a pioneer heroine is unquestioned. In 1791 what is today West Virginia was largely unsettled wilderness in the middle of a frontier war between would-be settlers and local Indian tribes.

When Fort Lee was threatened with attack and a low supply of ammunition, Annie Bailey, scout and messenger, rode alone through 100 miles of near wilderness to Fort Savannah at Lewisburg and returned with the needed powder to save the fort at Clendenin's Settlement which today is Charleston, West Virginia.

A poem was written in 1861 by Charles Robb about this ride. It was called – Annie Bailey's Ride.

Her career continued until 1795 and the signing of the Greenville Treaty to end the Indian Wars.

After John Bailey's death circa 1802 she made her home with her son but also travelled among her friends and was a welcome storyteller and trader.

In 1817 William moved his family across to Gallia County, Ohio, and Annie reluctantly left her beloved 'Virginia' to make a home near him, though she travelled still.

Even without the exaggerated stories, Annie Bailey was a unique and daring woman. She was certainly considered odd or outlandish, but she was also well-liked and respected on the frontier.

She died of old age on November 22, 1825 at home in Ohio aged 83.

An account written by the Artist Henry Howe in 1846:

'In my original visit to Gallipolis, Ohio, I failed of learning that the extraordinary specimen of humanity known as Mad Annie Bailey passed the latter part of her days in its vicinity. In my travels over Virginia in the years 1843-44 taking pencil sketches and collecting

materials for my work upon that State, I learned of her and inserted therein this account.'

There was an eccentric female, who lived in the Kanawha region towards the latter part of the last century. Her name was Ann Bailey. She was born in Liverpool, and had been the wife of an English soldier. She generally went by the name of 'Mad Annie'. During the wars with the Indians, she very often acted as a messenger, and conveyed letters from the fort, at Covington, to Point Pleasant. On these occasions she was mounted on a favourite horse of great sagacity, and rode like a man, with a rifle over her shoulder, and a tomahawk and a butcher's knife in her belt. At night she slept in the woods.

Her custom was to let her horse go free, and then walk some distance back on his trail, to escape being discovered by the Indians. After the Indian wars she spent some time in hunting. She pursued and shot deer and bears with the skill of a backwoodsman. She was a short, stout woman, very masculine and coarse in her appearance, and seldom or never wore a gown, but usually had on a petticoat, with a man's coat over it, and buckskin breeches. The services she rendered in the wars with the Indians endeared her to the people. 'Mad Annie', and her black pony 'Liverpool', were always welcome at every house.

Often, she gathered the honest, simple-hearted mountaineers around, and related her adventures and trials, while the sympathetic tear would course down their cheeks. She was profane, often became intoxicated, and could box with the skill of one of the fancy. 'Mad Annie' possessed considerable intelligence, and could read and write. She died in Ohio many years since.'

In this notice of her death which is copied by Mr. James Harper, from the Gallia Free Press, of December 3, 1825, published by his father. In a note with it he wrote: *'I saw Ann Bailey a short time before she died—the first and only time—and she made a lasting impression upon my six-year-old mind. She wore a hat, and her accoutrements were tomahawk and scalping knife.'* The account was published under the caption 'Longevity.'

'Died, in Harrison township, Gallia county, Ohio, on Tuesday, November 22, 1825, the celebrated Annie Bailey. According to her own story her father was a soldier in Queen Anne's war; that on getting a furlough to go home, he found his wife with a fine daughter in her arms, whom he called Ann, after the Queen, as a token of respect. In 1714 she went from Liverpool to London with her mother on a visit to her brother – while there, she saw Lord Lovett beheaded.

After she came to the United States she was married and the year after that her husband was killed at the battle of Point Pleasant in 1774; and so, to avenge his death, she joined the garrison, under the command of Col. Wm. Clendenin, where she remained until the final departure of the Indians from the country. She has always been noted for intrepid bravery. Col. Wm. Clendenin says, while he was commander of the garrison where Charleston, Kanawha, is now located, an attack by Indians was hourly expected. On examination it was believed that the ammunition on hand was insufficient to hold out a siege of any length; to send even two, three or four men to Lewisburg, the nearest place it could be had, a distance of 100 miles, was like sending men to be slaughtered; and to send a larger force was weakening the garrison. While in this state Annie Bailey volunteered to leave the fort in the night and go to Lewisburg. She did so—and travelled the wilderness, where not the vestige of a house was to be seen—arrived safe at Lewisburg, delivered her orders, received the ammunition, and returned safe to her post, amidst the plaudits of a grateful people.

In the April number, 1885, of the Magazine of Western History is a story of Mad Annie by Wm. P. Buell. It states that she was born in the year 1742, in Liverpool, England, and named in honour of Queen Anne, and was present with her parents at her coronation.

At the age of 30 she married John Trotter, who was killed at the battle of Point Pleasant in 1774. The loss of her husband filled her with rage and, swearing vengeance upon the entire savage race, she entered upon a career as a scout and spy. She hunted, rode and fought like a man.

She had a fine black horse called 'Liverpool', in honor of her birthplace, an animal of great beauty and intelligence. On one occasion, when she was pursued by Indians, she came to an impenetrable thicket where she was obliged to dismount and leave him for their capture. She then crawled into a hollow sycamore log. The Indians came and rested on the log, but without suspecting her concealment within.

After they had gone she followed their trail, and in the darkness of night recaptured the animal, and, mounting him, when at a safe distance from being shot or taken gave a shout of defiance and bounded away. The Indians eventually became afraid of her, regarding her as insane and therefore under the special protection of the Great Spirit.

In another account a James L. Newsom wrote about Mad Annie, he lived in a little cottage a stone's throw from the Ohio River. and was a boy of 14 when Mad Annie Bailey died. *'I knew Annie well,'* he said,

'She was a low-set, heavy woman, not over five feet two inches high, dressed in a petticoat

with a man's coat over it, wore a hat, and loved whiskey in her old age; often saw her come to town with a gun and a shot-pouch over her shoulder. She would not live with her son and grandchildren—was too wild. Her home was a cabin four miles below town, high on the Ohio river hills.

It was made like a shed, had one door and a single window, a small, four-pane affair. The roof was without nails, of black oak clapboards say four feet long, held to their places by weight poles. The only floor was the earth; she had no furniture, not even a bedstead. Mad Annie was passionate, high spirited, had excellent sense, would allow no trifling with her, and hated Indians.

She was very particular in the observance of the Sabbath; gathered in the children and taught them Sunday lessons. Her voice was coarse, like the growl of a lion, and she chewed tobacco like a pig, the saliva coming down the corners of her mouth.

I often saw her in town; she sometimes walked and sometimes paddled up in a canoe, and always with a gun and shot-pouch over her shoulder in hunter fashion.

Although spoken of as Mad Annie, no one ever had the temerity to so address her; the people fairly idolized her, treated her with great kindness, loaded her with presents and plied her well with whiskey. She died from old age, never was sick—only gave out.

She looked tough as a mule and seemed about as strong. I was a stout boy of 14 and one day she laid down her bundle of things which people gave her. We boys were afraid of her, as she was disposed to be a little cross, but as her back was turned I tried to lift it, but was unable. She lifted it with ease, and walked all the way to her home with it, four miles away.'

We are familiar with other real life women of the Wild West like Annie Oakley (Phoebe Anne Moses, 1860-1926) through the films 'Annie get your Gun' and 'Calamity Jane' (Martha Jane Cannary 1848-1903) - they were both born nearly a hundred years after the death of 'Mad Annie Bailey', in 1860 and 1848 respectively, and later became well known as show business performers.

Annie Bailey would probably have had both of them for breakfast.

CHAPTER NINE

Liverpool Ceramic Ware

During and after the American Revolution, a wide range of commemorative wares were produced for consumers in Britain and America, including Liverpool jugs, printed handkerchiefs, and China services.

People in Portsmouth, New Hampshire, paid tribute to the founding of the Republic by saving the artifacts commemorating the events and heroes of the Revolution.

Present day visitors to the town will see a wide variety of objects related to the American Revolution, including an extensive collection of Liverpool ceramics with patriotic motifs. These ceramics were made in Liverpool, England for the American market shortly after the Revolution.

Jugs made for export largely passed through the port city of Liverpool, which was also a major centre for manufacturing ceramic wares and for decorating wares made at other pottery producing districts.

It was common for American merchant seamen to order commemorative objects to be sent directly home or to be collected on their return voyage. During the early nineteenth century the Herculaneum Pottery in Toxteth, Liverpool dominated the American export trade. This was one of the most famous of Toxteth's industries and it produced high-quality earthenware and porcelain from about 1793 to 1841. 'This pottery, the largest ever established in Liverpool, was founded in 1796 on the site of some old copper works on the south shore of the River Mersey at Toxteth Park'.

The first productions were blue-printed wares. Dinner, toilet, tea, and coffee services, punch-bowls, mugs and jugs were made. This blue-printing may have been a practical adaption of what fate bestowed in the form of copper residues from Roe's works which are said to have tinged the early wares blue. Soon after cream-coloured ware, which was then fashionable was made and later, terracotta vases and other articles were produced. The cream-coloured or Queen's ware, is considered of fine quality and as well crafted as any available.

In 1833, the Herculaneum Pottery Company was officially dissolved and the property sold for £25,000 to Ambrose Lace.

The remaining stock was then sold, as a clipping the Liverpool Mercury Feb 22nd 1833 shows. Ambrose Lace in turn leased the premises to Thomas Case and James Mort, who carried on the business for three more years.

During this period a Liver bird was added to the factory markings. It was during their tenureship that a notable dinner service was made for the Corporation of Liverpool. It was blue-printed, and had on each piece the arms of Liverpool engraved.

In about 1836, Case, Mort and Co. was also dissolved to be succeeded by Mort & Simpson, who traded until the pottery finally closed in 1841 caused by competition from the Staffordshire potteries. This was the end of Liverpool's last pottery.

CHAPTER TEN

Liverpool Regiment in War of Independence

Banastre Tarleton
Painting by Sir Joshua Reynolds

A regiment was raised at the expense of the Port of Liverpool in January 1778, becoming one of many volunteer regiments formed during the American Revolutionary War.

In 1781, Banastre Tarleton was born to the merchant, ship owner and slave trader, John Tarleton of Liverpool (1719 – 1773), who was Mayor of Liverpool (1768).

General Sir Banastre Tarleton, (August 21, 1754 – January 25, 1833) was a British soldier and politician. As a young man, he had inherited £5,000 on his father's death, but squandered it all on gambling. In 1775 he purchased a commission as a cavalry officer in the 1st Dragoon Guards, and proved to be a gifted horseman and leader of troops.

His reputation for ruthlessness earned him the nickname 'Butcher' amongst American revolutionists. The British regarded him as an outstanding leader of light cavalry. On May 29, 1780 Tarleton, with a force of 150 soldiers on horseback, overtook a detachment of 350 to 380 Virginia Continentals led by Abraham Buford.

Buford refused to surrender, or even stop his march. Only after sustaining heavy casualties did Buford order the surrender. What happened next is cause of heated debate. According to American accounts, Tarleton mercilessly massacred his prisoners. In the end, more Americans were sabred to death in what became known as the Waxhaw massacre.

In recounting Tarleton's action at the scene one member of the British Army who was there, a surgeon named Robert Brownfield, wrote that 'Tarleton was in the midst of them, when commenced a scene of indiscriminate carnage, never surpassed by the ruthless atrocities of the most barbarous savages.'

The Waxhaw massacre became an important rallying cry for the revolutionaries.

The Regiment returned to Liverpool in early 1784, where it was disbanded following Britain's defeat in the American Revolution.

In 1784, Tarleton stood for election as MP for Liverpool, but was narrowly defeated. In 1790 he succeeded Richard Pennant as MP for Liverpool in the Parliament of Great Britain and, with the exception of a single year, remained in the House of Commons until 1812.

Tarleton spoke on military matters and a variety of other subjects, but especially the slave trade, with which the port of Liverpool was particularly associated.

In reality, Tarleton was working to preserve the slavery business of his brothers Clayton and Thomas, and he became well-known for his taunting and mockery of the abolitionists.

In 1815, he was made a Baronet and in 1820 a Knight Grand Cross of the Order of the Bath .

Despite being married to an illegitimate daughter of the 4th Duke of Ancaster since 1798, he lived with the actress Mary Robinson (Perdita), whom he seduced to win a bet.

Despite their 15 year relationship, they had no children, although in 1783 Robinson had a miscarriage.

Banastre Tarleton died childless at Leintwardine, Shropshire, England in 1833.

The Hollywood movie The Patriot (2000) controversially portrayed a character (Colonel William Tavington played by Jason Isaacs) based on Tarleton as a cruel, sadistic commander who massacred prisoners of war and innocent civilians.

Banastre Tarleton is also portrayed in the 2006 film Amazing Grace (played by Ciarán Hinds) as the main opponent in the British Parliament to the slave trade abolitionists, led by William Wilberforce.

Tarleton Street in Liverpool carries the family name into posterity.

CHAPTER ELEVEN

Liverpool
and the American Civil War

War broke out in April 1861. The civil war divided America between the Northern Union States and Southern Confederate States. There were many causes for the war, although they centred on slavery and State rights.

At this time 60% of the Confederate States' cotton was coming through Liverpool – once the Northern ships began blocking their passage this had a huge impact upon trade within Liverpool.

Liverpool also made a large amount of money directly from the Slave Trade, which the Confederates supported.

In October 1864, Liverpool staged a bazaar at St George's Hall called the 'Southern Prisoners' Relief Fund'. It lasted for five days and raised over £20,000.

St. George's Hall, Liverpool

James Dunwoody Bulloch

James Dunwoody Bulloch was born on the 25th June 1823 near Savannah, Georgia.

At 16 James joined the U.S. Navy and quickly rose to the rank of Lieutenant, but soon he hit a ceiling and needing money for his family he resigned his commission and took up service with the Cromwell Steam Company.

At the outbreak of the Civil war in 1861 he was in command of a passenger mail ship, Bienville, which he was asked to sell to the Confederates. He refused but promised to resign his commission and join in their campaign.

When he arrived at his next destination, New York, and saw that his passengers were Union soldiers who were traveling to the south to put down the rebellion, he resigned immediately and reported to the Confederate States Navy department to sign up. His task was to procure ships from Europe for use in the battles.

Mr Bulloch was sent by Stephen Malloy (Secretary of the Confederate States Navy Department) to Liverpool to purchase, and or, build ships for use by the navy.

Under English law it was illegal for UK companies to supply armed war vessels to warring factions.

Bulloch was sent to acquire ships without being caught breaking the law.

Captain Bulloch arrived in Liverpool on 4th June 1861, and set up his Liverpool H.Q. at 10 Rumford Place, near to the Town Hall.

He enlisted the help of a number of people in his attempt to purchase vessels: George Alfred Trenholme acted as a banker for the Confederates and enabled James to circumvent certain paperwork which may have linked the purchases to the confederates.

10 Rumford Place

A Mr. F. Hull, a local solicitor, who advised him that he could purchase ships as a private individual without infringing the 'British Enlistment' providing they weren't equipped for war.

Knowing that the Confederacy was desperate for arms and cash, he quickly arranged for the construction of two fast and powerful cruisers, CSS *Florida* and CSS *Alabama*, these were built at Cammel Lairds shipyard, Birkenhead and destined to prey upon the Union's merchant shipping. James' brother, Irvine, would serve and fight on the CSS *Alabama*.

Capt Bulloch was also involved in constructing and acquiring a number of other warships and blockade runners for the Confederacy. Meanwhile, Bulloch, under near-constant surveillance by Northern agents in downtown Liverpool, was investigated by a number of men who tried to prove he was purchasing war ships but he managed to stay ahead of them.

Liver Hotel, Waterloo

LIVER HOTEL - Waterloo

So he began the recruitment of Liverpool based seamen for the crewing of the 'CSS *Alabama*' at the Liver Hotel, South Road, Waterloo. It is thought that Bulloch also held meetings here with Captain Ralph Sammes – The Master of the Confederate ship 'CSS *Alabama*'.

However Bulloch really wanted to return to commanding ships but he proved too valuable in his current role and was beaten to the command of the '*Enrica*' (renamed the 'CSS *Alabama*') by Captain

Raphael Semmes. Captain James Dunwoody Bulloch lived at a number of different houses in the Waterloo area of Crosby near Liverpool in an effort to avoid detection by agents of the U S Government, including Marine Terrace and a number of addresses in Wellington Street.

Another Waterloo landmark - The Royal Hotel was used by Confederate Naval Officers for recuperation after illness or injuries.

James Dunwoody Bulloch (25 June 1823 – 7 January 1901) was the Confederate States of America's chief foreign agent in Great Britain during the American Civil War. Bulloch was never pardoned for his role in the war and became a British citizen employed as

Clifton House (above) in Cambridge Road, is now a Children's Day Nursery.

a cotton trader and died at 76 Canning Street, Liverpool, the home of his son-in-law Alderman Maxwell Hyslop Maxwell in Liverpool on 7th January 1901 and is buried in Toxteth cemetery. In his will he left $30,000 to his nephew, Theodore, soon to become the 26th US President.

Toxteth Cemetery, Liverpool

On his grave marker is the inscription, 'an American by birth, an Englishman by choice.'

The 26 sixth U.S. President Theodore Roosevelt wrote in his autobiography.

'My mother's two brothers, James Dunwoody Bulloch and Irvine Bulloch, came to visit us shortly after the close of the war. Both came under assumed names, as they were among the Confederates who were at that time exempted from the amnesty. Uncle Jimmy Bulloch was a dear old retired sea-captain, utterly unable to get on in the worldly sense of that phrase, as valiant and simple and upright a soul as ever lived, He was an Admiral in the Confederate navy, and was the builder of the famous Confederate war vessel Alabama. My uncle Irvine Bulloch was a midshipman on the Alabama, and fired the last gun discharged from her batteries in the fight with the Kearsarge. Both of these uncles lived in Liverpool after the war.'

A convoluted link – James Dunwoody Bulloch was the halfbrother of a distinguished Confederate naval officer, Irvine Bulloch and of Martha Bulloch. Martha was the mother of future U.S. President Theodore Roosevelt and the grandmother of Eleanor Roosevelt, who in turn became the wife of Franklin Delano Roosevelt the 32nd President of the United States.

During World War Two the war time American Presidents wife Eleanor Roosevelt, made a secret visit to American military camps in and around Liverpool as a morale booster.

Consider Bulloch's activities along Liverpool's dock area during the American Civil War,and eighty years later, the visit to the same Docks by his sister Martha's Granddaughter, Mrs Roosevelt during World War Two. Same Location, Same Family, Different War, Strange coincidence.

For further details of this see pages – 75/76.

President Abraham Lincoln

As one of the early repercussions of the defeat of the confederates in the Civil War, President Lincoln was assassinated at Ford's Theatre, Washington in 1865 by John Wilkes Booth, just days after the surrender of the Confederates.

John Wilkes Booth's father, Junius Booth, a Shakespearean actor, is said to have come from Liverpool.

However Junius Brutus Booth – actor, was born in London on the 1st May 1796 and died November 1852.

He was the son of Richard Booth, a lawyer, and Jane Elizabeth Game. He was also grandson of John Booth, a silversmith, and Elizabeth Wilkes, a relative of the English radical and politician John Wilkes.

Junius Booth later became a popular actor at Liverpool's Theatre Royal which opened 1772 at Williamson Square. It is probably this connection which has led to him being described as born in Liverpool.

The British-born actor who as a young man, fell in love with a flower girl named Mary Ann Holmes.

Junius Booth

However he was already married and had a son, but he decided to escape such inconveniences by running off with Mary Ann to Baltimore, USA in 1821, where he continued his acting career.

Junius Booth became a famous actor on the American stage, and he became notorious for his drunkenness, eccentricities, and instabilities.

Mary Ann Holmes did not formally marry Junius Booth until 1851, but she bore him ten children.

One of which was John Wilkes Booth, who was born in 1838, and would later become the infamous assassin of President Lincoln.

Another of Richard Booth's sons was Algernon Sidney Booth 1798 - 1803, and it is this Booth who was the great-great-great-grandfather of Cherie (nee Booth) Blair.

Anthony Booth - born in Waterloo near Liverpool in 1937.

After attending the local Catholic Grammar School, St Marys College, he served his compulsory National Service in the Army, and developed a taste for acting while serving in Paris. He spent five years honing his acting skills in repertory theatre, before venturing into films and television in the 1960s. He has played roles in over twenty films

His great great grandfather was Algernon Booth whose nephew was John Wilkes Booth, infamous for being President Abraham Lincoln's assassin.

To quote from a description of his great-great Uncle Junius *'He became a famous actor on the stage, notorious for his drunkenness, eccentricities, and instabilities.'*

What is remarkable here is the line of connection between President Abraham Lincoln and British Prime Minister Blair.

Anthony Booth is the father of Cherie Booth.

So what has this to do with the British Prime Minister, Tony Blair?

For those who may be unaware, the wife of the British Prime Minister was formerly Cherie Booth.

She shares with John Wilkes Booth a common line of descent from one Richard Booth and Elizabeth Game.

American Civil War: The Final Twist

The first shot of the civil war was fired by a gun built in Duke Street Liverpool, and the last act of the Civil War was the surrender made in Liverpool Town Hall on the 6th November 1865, when the CSS *Shenandoah* travelled from San Francisco to Liverpool.

At 220 feet long and 32.5 feet wide, the *'Shenandoah'* weighed 1,018 tons and was propeller-driven by a 250-horsepower steam engine with a top speed of eight knots.

That speed could be doubled with the use of sails. She was armed with two 32-pounders and six 68-pounders.

The newly commissioned CSS *Shenandoah*, set out on October 19 on a 58,000 mile 'round-the-world' cruise under the command of Capt. James Waddell.

On the way to Melbourne, Australia, where they arrived on January 25, 1865, Waddell and his crew burned seven Yankee ships and ransomed two.

After refitting and taking on more crew, the CSS *Shenandoah* sailed north into the Pacific, capturing four more ships by the end of May.

The CSS *Shenandoah* sailed into Sea of Alaska and then into the Arctic Ocean. There she found the bulk of the Northern United States Whaling fleet. She sank them all and thus, this lone Confederate Raider changed the way that the entire world lit its night. In less than 18 months, the CSS *Shenandoah* sunk a total of 36 Union merchant and commerce ships.

CSS Shenandoah

There was no way for Waddell and his crew to know that the Confederate states had lost their bid for independence and that the raider was now fighting for a cause that was already lost.

Not until August 2nd did Waddell find out from a British vessel that the war was over.

Afraid that the United States might hang him as a pirate, Captain Waddell stowed the ship's guns and set out from San Francisco on a 17,000-mile voyage to England.

On November 6th 1865, the CSS *Shenandoah* sailed into Liverpool, and the Captain of the CSS *Shenandoah* surrendered at Liverpool Town Hall to the British Government rather than to the American Union Government.

From the Liverpool Mercury 10th November 1865

The Confederate Ship *Shenandoah*

The following letter is addressed to Earl Russell by Capt. Waddell,

'*To the Right Hon. Earl Russell, H.B.M. Minister for Foreign Affairs.*' November 5th

I have the honour to announce to your lordship my arrival in the waters of the Mersey with this vessel, lately a ship of war in my command, belonging to the Confederate States of America.

Capt. Waddell

I think that as all the property of the Confederate Government has reverted, by the fortune of war, to the Government of the United States of North America. I have, therefore, sought this port as a suitable one and, if I am without a Government, to surrender the ship, with her battery, small arms, stores, tackle, and apparel complete to Her Majesty's Government, for such disposition as in its wisdom should be deemed proper.

I have the honour to be, very respectfully, your lordship's obedient servant,

James. I. Waddell, Commander.

CSS Shenandoah

Capt Waddell

CHAPTER TWELVE

World War One

America did not particularly want to engage in the Great War as the United States included many people of English, French, and German ancestry, so it was difficult for many Americans to choose sides. The American people had a strong feeling of isolationism, believing that they should not become entangled in foreign wars.

Many U.S. citizens were enraged when a German submarine sunk the British transatlantic liner, Lusitania.

More than 1200 passengers boarded the luxury ship sailing from New York to the port of Liverpool, which was also home to most of the crew.

On May 7, 1915, the Germans torpedoed and sunk the Lusitania. Of the nearly 1200 deceased 128 were Americans.

A later investigation showed the hull of the ship was filled with weapons to be used against Germany. Many Americans urged President Wilson to join the war. When World War I broke out, Lusitania was making monthly sailings between Liverpool and New York. However, on 7 May 1915, while heading east off the Old Head of Kinsale, Ireland, Lusitania was torpedoed without warning by U-20 and sank within 18 minutes. Two explosions rocked the ship. The first was clearly caused by a torpedo from U-20. The cause of the second explosion has never been definitively determined and remains the source of much controversy.

Of those on board, 761 were rescued, while 1,198 perished.

During the First World War (1914-1918), Liverpool was the premier strategic port of Britain's 'Western Approaches'.

Hundreds of convoys sailed to and from the port, braving the deadly U-boat threat, in order to keep Britain supplied with food and other essentials for the war effort.

America finally joined the Allies by declaring war on Germany in April 1917, and almost immediately sent a large contingent of troops to Europe.

General Pershing landed at Liverpool with his US armies in June 1917.

Liverpool was the first port of call for the American forces on their way to assist the British Army to achieve victory over Germany.

As well as stores, weapons and equipment which where shipped through the port in huge amounts, Hundreds of thousands of US soldiers landed here on their way to the trenches in France.

An eye witness account from the 71st Artillery US Army - in 1917,wrote in a letter home.

'Early in the morning of August 13 we picked up our destroyer escort consisting of the USS Terry. Our men greeted the ships flying the American flag and manned by our own blue jackets, with prolonged cheers.

On Thursday August 15, we sailed into Liverpool, with flags flying and the band playing on the deck for the first time since leaving Halifax.'

A massive transit camp was set up at Knotty Ash, and here after marching the five miles from the Pier Head, they would await shipment by rail to south coast ports en route to France

American doughboys marching up the 'Floating Roadway' at the Landing Stage, Pier Head, Liverpool. New York Times October 1918.

Both sections of the Regiment disembarked from their respective transports in the afternoon and marched independently to the American rest camp at Knotty Ash, where for the first time the Regiment was united.

Centre fold images information.

The images shown in the centre pages of this book are unique have not been shown to the public before, as they were the property of Colonel Dorris Hanes, United States Army.

They were commissioned by the US military during world war two, largely to record the visit to the Unit in Liverpool by the war time American Presidents Wife; Mrs Eleanor Roosevelt.

The images were part of an archive in the University of Texas which has stored them since the end of world war two.

During Franklin D. Roosevelt's presidency, Eleanor Roosevelt was an active First Lady who travelled extensively around the nation, visiting relief projects, surveying working and living conditions, and then reporting her observations to the President.

She also exercised her own political and social influence; she became an advocate of the rights and needs of the poor, of minorities, and of the disadvantaged.

In World War II, she visited England and the South Pacific to foster good will among the Allies and boost the morale of US servicemen overseas. In 1942, she accepted an invitation to visit England to see what British women were doing for the war effort and to convey a message of support from her husband to the American troops stationed there.

While in England she visited several American Red Cross service clubs and noted that they were much appreciated by American GIs.

It was on this visit to American troops in Liverpool that the photographs in the centre fold pages were taken.

Blitz Park.
US Army open storage at Liverpool Docks

US Army Camp at Deyes Lane Maghull
Mrs Roosevelt meets US Army corporal.

Stanley Dock Warehouse

Officers in a specially adapted Jeep which was able to be used around the building via the goods lift.

Liverpool dockers unload Barges which were used to move goods from ships at the dockside

US Army and Liverpool civilians working at main administration offices at Castle Street in central Liverpool

US plane transporters passing Water Street Liverpool after being unloaded at the Pier Head 1942

American soldiers checking stocks at Stanley Warehouse

Liverpool dock workers moving goods around the building. Dockers and other British civilians were used to handle goods and supplies under the supervision of American personnel

Chart showing civilian dock workers who were employed by US Forces and their locations on the Mersey Docks system

Mrs Eleanor Roosevelt, wife of wartime US President.
Accompanied by US Army Area Commander Colonel D Hanes talks with US Army Sergeant
at Stanley Warehouse, November 1942

Mrs Eleanor Roosevelt meets Liverpool dock workers on her tour of Stanley Warehouse facility, 1942

American 40s Film Star Adolphe Menjou shown here with Colonel Hanes, visiting troops at a wartime Military Hospital

While at Knotty Ash Camp, every officer and enlisted man was presented with a letter of welcome from King George'.

Former US Army Camp Huts at Knotty Ash Used as accommodation by Liverpool Corporation Housing after the first World War.

The whole camp site was bought by the City Council in 1932 and converted into a Liverpool municipal housing estate.

This image is from the 'NEW YORK TIMES' in 1915 - before the entry of the U.S. into the War and shows a wives and relatives of Liverpool Soldiers at The Front, who have joined the Women's Reserves for Home Defence, being drilled in a school yard in Liverpool.'

Liverpool was the first port of call for the American forces on their way to assist the British Army to achieve victory over Germany.

As well as stores, weapons and equipment which where shipped through the port in huge amounts, hundreds of thousands of US soldiers landed here on their way to the trenches in France.

The First World War spanned four years and involved many nation states.

1918 was to be the final year of the war. This year saw the German military high command attempt one final large-scale offensive on the Western Front. A near success, but an ultimate failure which led to an increasing series of successes by the Allies from the summer of 1918.

By the autumn, the German Army was no longer able to continue fighting. Germany's political leadership petitioned for an armistice.

It took effect at 11am on 11 November – the eleventh hour of the eleventh day of the eleventh month. The war was over, and with its end many of the European dynasties fell.

An extract from the US Army newspaper 'Stars and Stripes' – in November 1918 describes the repatriation of American troops from France back to the US. Almost all available vessels were reserved by the United States for this operation and meant that Canadian and other commonwealth troops were delayed in the UK for almost twelve months. This eventually led to riots and even mutiny amongst the Canadians.

'20,000 American soldiers have sailed from Liverpool, England for the United States, since the armistice. Some of these have been in England for only eight months.

The first to go were assembled at a camp in Knotty Ash near Liverpool where some thousands of Americans spent their first night on foreign soil. There are streets too, and sidewalks, and an adequate draining system but there is still mud when it rains.

Knotty Ash, before the war a cluster of semi-detached cottages, is now one of the boom towns of the US Army Expeditionary Forces.

Queens Drive, which is one of Liverpool's main thoroughfares, is just one US army truck after another, on its way to the docks at Liverpool, and every truck is piled high with Kit bags issued, but never used.'

['Stars & Stripes' – November 1918]

World War One was the catalyst for the decline of Britain's global domination as a colonial super power.

Conversely, America began its ascent to the position of global number one, economically as well as militarily.

The sinking of the RMS Laurentic in January 1917 off the coast of Donegal, one of countless ships which were sunk by the Germans during the 1914 - 1918 conflict, underlines how much the war cost in financial terms.

What made this vessel distinctly different was its cargo of 3,211 bars of gold bullion.

In late 1916, the British Treasury was preparing to send tens of millions in gold across the Atlantic. The United States had not then declared war on Germany. But American as well as Canadian factories were working twenty-four hours a day to make munitions for Great Britain and her Allies, and those munitions had to be paid for.

RMS Laurentic

So in January, 1917, the gold was sent from H.M. Treasury to Liverpool, where it was loaded into the second class baggage room of the Laurentic.

On 25 January, 1917, the former passenger liner, Laurentic converted to armed merchant cruiser, after a short stop at Buncrana in Donegal, sailed for Halifax, Nova Scotia. On board were 475 people.

Also on board were 3,211 gold ingots, a payment from the British Government to the U.S. Government for armaments and supplies. At today's values the ingots would be worth almost £300m. As the ship rounded Malin Head it hit two German mines.

The rough seas and extreme cold took its toll. Many of the dead in the boats were frozen solid. The 14,892 ton ship went down in 45 minutes.

Only 121 of the 475 aboard survived. But the story of Laurentic doesn't end there. Many sunken ships are the subject of rumours about treasure being on board, but Laurentic is one of the relatively few cases where there actually was treasure.

In addition to her passengers and crew, the ship was carrying 3,211 bars of gold bullion. In what Anderson describes as 'one of the world's most amazing salvage operations,' Royal Navy divers made some 5,000 dives to the wreck between 1917 and 1924. At a significant cost, they succeeded in recovering all but about 25 of the bars. The Royal Navy returned to the site in 1952 to recover the rest.

Many Britons felt that the US loans should be considered as part of its contribution to the World War I effort. The loan, which was twice as large as the British economy at the time, had a 2% interest rate and required annual payments.

It was used to buy oil, food, arms and military equipment.

'Even more striking is the post-war ascendancy of the United States. It is the great gainer by the war, financially, industrially and politically. It has gathered in Europe's gold, in payment for war supplies; it is the creditor of the States of Europe and takes ruthless political advantage of its financial superiority ...

Financial power has further immensely increased American commerce; while British exports to all parts of the world have fallen, American have gone up.

Where Germany has been driven from the field it has been to the advantage, not of Britain, but of America and Japan.

While American industry expands, British industry, in its vital sections (coal, cotton), contracts. America has become the greatest financial magnate in the world.

Wilhelm Dibelius, A German economist writing about Britain (1921).

CHAPTER THIRTEEN

World War Two

Pier Head, Liverpool

The Second World War began on September 3, 1939, after Germany invaded Poland, using the false pretext of a faked 'Polish attack' on a German border post. The United Kingdom and France gave Germany two days to withdraw from Poland. Once the deadline passed, the United Kingdom, Australia, and New Zealand declared war on Germany.

Two years later, the US declared war on Japan on 8th December, 1941 after the Japanese attack on Pearl Harbour.

On 11th December 1941. Germany and Italy declared war on the United States, which brought the US into the European Theatre of Operations.

The US 8th Army Airforce began arriving in the United Kingdom during the late Spring of 1942, with the US Army arriving later in the year.

Liverpool's role in the Second World War (1939-1945) was crucial. Her importance as a convoy destination was second to none in that she maintained a lifeline, with the USA and Canada which was vital to Britain's survival, and eventual victory.

Much of the 'Battle of the Atlantic' against the U-boats was indeed, fought and won from Liverpool.

Scene of destruction at the junction of Lord Street and Castle Street in May 1941, after German Raid

Liverpool's importance to the allied war effort was clear to Hitler, who ordered his Luftwaffe to 'destroy' the port.

During the war, Liverpool was subjected to more bombing raids (68) than any British city outside London, the worst being the terrible 8-night 'May Blitz' of 1941.

Between 1940 and 1942, nearly 4,000 Merseysiders were killed and 4,000 seriously injured in these raids, which did immense damage to the port and city. But despite this devastation, the work of the port continued.

As well as food and war supplies, hundreds of thousands of American and Canadian troops were transported to Britain via Liverpool in readiness for the Allied landings in Normandy, which led to the German defeat in Western Europe.

Liverpool had two other vital roles to perform in World War Two.

As the headquarters of the Battle of the Atlantic operation and as the first link in a chain of transportation and distribution from the United States, of vast quantities of equipment, food, munitions and aircraft needed for the Allied War effort.

On 10th February, USS Wakefield was re-commissioned and she departed Boston on 13th April, beginning the first of 23 round-trips in the Atlantic theater, and three in the Pacific. Wakefield operated as a 'lone wolf,' except for air coverage a few miles out of a port. Her primary

USS Wakefield

port of call in the European theater was Liverpool – visited so often in fact that the transport's crew nicknamed her 'The Boston and Liverpool Ferry.'

The average round-trip voyage took 18 days. After D-day, 6th June 1944, Wakefield began the first of her trips as a casualty evacuation ship, bringing home wounded GI's. Between 13 April 1944 and 1st February 1946, Wakefield transported 110,563 troops to Europe and brought some 106,674 men back to America – a total of 217,237 passengers.

The only visible sign of the presence of American military personnel in Liverpool during the Second World War is a large stone plaque, which was installed in the wall of the former floating roadway at the Pier Head, Liverpool in 1944, and reads:

> HERE IN THE DARK DAYS OF WAR AND IN THE DAWN OF VICTORY AMERICAN TROOPS AND CARGOES MOVED THROUGH THIS PORT FURTHERED BY BRITISH AND AMERICANS WORKING TOGETHER THIS STONE RECORDS THEIR UNITY IN ACCOMPLISHING THEIR MISSION. ERECTED BY THE 15TH PORT UNIT. US ARMY. 1944

Ralph Boyd, US Army veteran was based in Liverpool during World War Two with the 15th Port Unit, and sent an account of his wartime service in Liverpool in a letter to the author in May 2006.

Mr & Mrs Ralph Boyd, by the Plaque installed in the wall of the floating roadway, Pier Head in 1999

'We landed in Glasgow, Scotland on December 15, 1943, and were then taken to Liverpool by train. They would bus us each day from Kirkby to Liverpool so we could work on the docks with the 15th Port Mobil T.C. (Transportation Corps) our job was to supervise the unloading and the shipping of supplies to other depots for the troops on the line.

71

We worked about 27 miles of dock at Liverpool and Birkenhead sometimes the Navy would let us sleep overnight on the ships so we could work longer and save time being shuttled back and forth.

The average age of the people working on the docks was 45 to 60 since most of the young men were in service. They were very good people to work with and very hard workers.

Sometimes we worked as many as six to seven ships at a time. This kept you pretty busy riding the overhead from one dock to the other. We sometimes had to depend on the civilians to keep track of the material shipped because we were so busy.

In September 1999, we went to England with my sister-in-law and her husband to visit their son and his family. They took us to Liverpool. Here we saw the acknowledgement for the help from the 15th Port USA at Princes Gate Pier. I knew this had been put up, and was very happy to find it.'

During 1942 there began to appear a growing number of US Army and US Army Airforce bases in and around Liverpool the best known being the huge Airforce Base at Burtonwood.

Burtonwood Air Base opened in 1941, just in time to supply Spitfires for the Battle of Britain, and was probably the biggest military base in Europe during the war.

With a peak of 18,063 personnel, this site had a massive impact on the area as a whole.

US Aircrew at Burtonwood

There were also a number of smaller depots, most of which are now almost forgotten.

At Haydock, Merseyside - US Base number 530. Combat Support Wing. A maintenance unit probably serving US Air Force at Burtonwood.

At Maghull - US Base number 577. Deyes Lane Camp, Maghull, Lancashire. 3989 Quartermasters Truck Regiment, 7th Air Force Service Command. A segregated vehicle maintenance unit composed of African American troops, with white officers, serving the Liverpool area.

At Kirkby – US Base number 514. Kirkby, Lancashire. Port Intransit Depot Number 2. The admin building at the entrance to the present day Industrial Estate, served as an American Officers Mess.

At Aintree Racecourse – US Base number 1960. Aintree, Lancashire. Ordnance Depot Company (Aviation), a large vehicle storage and ordnance facility with over 1600 US military personnel.

At Huyton – US Base Number 1511 Quartermaster Truck Regiment. Air Service Command.

At Southport Palace Hotel - US Base number 524. US Officers' Convalescence Facility.

At Silcocks Warehouse - US Base number 1. Port Transit Depot. Transformed during the Second World War from a grain warehouse to an aircraft spares facility.

At Stanley Dock Warehouse - US Base number 1. Port Transit Depot. Situated on the Dock Road, Liverpool, it was built in 1901 and was at the time, the biggest brick building in the world. It became the Liverpool logistics base for the US army.

US stores being loaded into Stanley Dock Warehouse

In conjunction with the Silcocks Warehouse nearby, this facility was responsible for the storage and shipment of large quantities of food, garments, medical supplies and a thousand and one articles needed to maintain a large army at war.

Headquarters

General Depot G-14
United States Army.
Liverpool.

4th December 1942

Page 3, APPENDIX 'A'

Stanley Warehouse.

This warehouse consists of eleven floors for warehousing with the ground floor designated as quay and one bay set aside for the cooperage* All warehousing, inventorying, checking and record keeping is done by civilians and each floor has a civilian in charge who keeps a record of supplies on hand and its location on the floor*

This warehouse contains C & E sales store and subsistence and regular supplies.

The Quay —The ground floor ie reserved for incoming and outgoing shipments. Incoming supplies are tallied-in from rail wagons, trucks, horse drays and barges by civilian checkers from weighbills, railroad notes or wagon bills

The Cooperage — is also located on the quay and all damaged cases, supplies incoming and out going are transferred from warehouse proper, and sent to this department for repacking.

Subsistence Depot – Is situated on the first floor and contains a model stock for over 200,000 men for a two weeks period.

The perishables and cold stores records are also maintained at main office, and are in fairly good condition.

Stanley Annexe –a small separate Warehouse containing C & E supplies and is considered a break down depot. The stock wreck code cards are maintained here and inventories are taken by the same civilian personnel who keep the code accounts. The supplies are tallied in from Stanley warehouse as

an inter- warehouse operation and issues are made to units on packing list prepared by a main office.

Sandon Warehouse.

This warehouse contains sales store supplies and is divided into a bowl and distribution depot.

Blitz Park

This is an open storage lot containing equipment. The stock records are maintained here as well as tally records. But supplies are in process of being transferred from this area to Stanley warehouse.

Main Office.

This is situated in Castle Street, Liverpool. From here all administration for the above depots is carried out by civilian and Army personnel.

Mrs. Eleanor Roosevelt inspecting the Stanley Dock Warehouse in November 1942

Mrs. Eleanor Roosevelt inspecting one of the American troops based at the Stanley Dock Warehouse in November 1942

This secret visit in 1942 by the US President Roosevelt's wife was made to the UK to help boost troop morale and bolster UK/US relations.

(These photos and information have been archived in the US for the last 60 years and only recently obtained by the author)

During World War Two, African-American troops were based in segregated camps and the camp at Maghull was no exception to the rule. Mrs Roosevelt a supporter of the early Civil Rights Movement, was known to be opposed to segregation and often went out of her way to visit Black troops, insofar as she could.

Mrs Roosevelt inspecting African American Troops at US Camp in Deyes Lane Maghull

Memories of local people in Maghull about the US Army Camp.

'*I was informed by locals, that a unit of African-American Servicemen, were in fact stationed at a camp that is now the Pumping Station, situated between Lydiate and Formby, on Altcar Road near to Tesco's in Formby. They used to frequent the old Coach and Horses pub, which is now the Office Suppliers and a Chemist, which is just a few doors down from the new Coach and Horses in Southport Road, Maghull.*

Apparently the camp stretched over as far as Poverty Lane, and up to Moss Lane. There was also a Cinema on the camp. The Yanks also used to play cricket and football with the locals on the King George V playing fields. After the war the camp was used by Polish soldiers and refugees'.

(Information supplied by Charles Wesley Southern)

American troops marching in the Victory Parade, which took place in Liverpool Road South, Maghull in 1945.

Images by kind permission of Dr. J.K. Rowlands

Looking at these images of American servicemen I wondered about the men, and how many of their ancestors were transported from Africa to America on ships which were owned by Liverpool based slave traders. Probably most of them.

How ironic that these men after generations of poor treatment in the U.S. volunteered to travel to the aid Britain in her hour of need, and then to be based in the city which was instrumental in the process of uprooting their ancestors and carrying them against their will across the ocean to slavery in America.

Pier Head - Transporting Airplanes to Lockheed, Speke

Plane travelling past Water Street and Town Hall

Convoy travelling up Parliament Street

Breeze Hill - Queens Drive

Photos courtesy of Burtonwood Association

The preceding images are of US war planes which have been unloaded from the deck of a large US sea going vessel, and craned ashore for transportation along a specially prepared route to Lockheed Aircraft facility at Speke.

They are seen passing the Liver Buildings, at the junction of Water Street, on vehicle transporters. The former Liverpool Overhead Railway can be seen behind the tramcars.

They were then taken by road to Speke Airport, on the fringe of Liverpool, where they were re-erected and commissioned prior to being flown to the US base at Warton near Preston for final delivery to US Bases across the UK.

Aintree Racecourse – BADA Aintree Lancashire Det A, 1960 Ordnance Depot Co. Aintree has long been internationally known as being the home of the Grand National Steeplechase.

Did you know that it has also been home to an aircraft factory, an armaments factory, a French Navy camp and a huge US Army camp? Late in 1943 the site was used as a base for thousands of US Army soldiers and airmen, in preparation for D-Day.

It became a link to the docks at Liverpool, where supplies and equipment arrived aboard merchant ships sailing from America, and carried in convoys across the Atlantic.

Tanks, vehicles, and equipment, that were to be used in the Invasion of France on D Day, were transported by road from the docks to Aintree. The whole of the racecourse site became a gigantic vehicle park. At the end of the war, the American forces departed as quickly as they had arrived, and the Racecourse slowly returned back to normal, leaving hardly a trace behind.

It was 1942 and I was then five years old, suddenly every thing changed in North Liverpool. The American Army arrived and overnight everything seemed to change from black and white to colour.

I was reminded of this event, which happened over 60 years ago, when I was visiting my daughter and her family in Utah, USA earlier this year.

I was in a small town called Ogden visiting the local railway museum, and talking to one of the guides who mentioned that the Union Pacific Station there had been at the crossroads of the many wartime military training camps in the area. It was from here that many US soldiers would set out on the first leg of their long journey to Britain and begin their preparations for the invasion of Europe on D Day.

It prompted me to think about my own memories of those times in 1942, when a succession of troop ships arrived at Liverpool Pierhead Landing Stage.

I can still clearly remember thousands of GI's marching in columns along Walton Vale, as I came out of school. They were followed by enormous trucks, jeeps, tankers and every conceivable type of military vehicle.

They were marching from the docks to take up residence at the world famous Aintree Racecourse — the home of the Grand National.

Eventually over 16,000 of them were camped there, with the racecourse turned into a vast parking lot for military vehicles and equipment.

Memories of individuals like the GI who was walking towards my sister and I as we walked home from school along Moss Lane , he was carrying a large box of chocolates in a box tied up with a ribbon. He asked if we liked candy — 'What is it ?' we said, then quickly added, 'Yes please'. He had obviously failed to impress one of the local girls, but certainly impressed us.

Of the time when a trio of musicians in uniform came into our classroom and mercifully relieved us from our boredom by playing some swing music.

How they never seemed to tire of being asked countless times 'Got any gum chum' by hordes of kids.

The Americans soon took over the area, especially cafes, milk bars and pubs and dance halls.

One of them, the Aintree Institute, later became more well known as one of the venues of The Beatles in the sixties.

Liverpool is fondly remembered by many U.S. servicemen who were stationed at bases around the city, such as Aintree and Haydock. But the biggest U.S. base was Burtonwood, around ten miles outside Liverpool, which still housed tens of thousands at the height of the Cold War in the 1950s and 1960s. Consequently many 'GI brides' originated from Merseyside.

A plaque was erected at the Pier Head Liverpool to commemorate the fact that over a million US soldiers passed through the port on their way to take part in D- day.

Many would later return in one of the thousands of military coffins stored in a requisitioned warehouse on the waterfront.

But that was a part of the war I was yet to discover. After the heavy bombing which had already devastated large parts of the city during the May Blitz of 1941, the war had now became an exhilarating and colourful experience for us small boys, with the continuing excitement of so many new people and events happening almost daily all around us.

It now appears to me that all the pain and suffering that brought about the eventual victory over the enemy will eventually be forgotten - what lasts is the bonds of our common humanity.

Now whenever I pass the racecourse at Aintree, I recall those times 60 years ago when Little America came to visit in 1943, and then quietly went back home in 1945. and of the many little acts of kindness which these strange and colourful allies brought to our community during those dark and dangerous times.

JP Kerrigan. 2004.

(An extract from the BBC 'Peoples War' web site.)

The war finally ended in 1945 and so did the US military presence in Liverpool.

Lets hope it stays that way in the future.

CHAPTER FOURTEEN

Cultural Links

Liverpool Waterfront

Liverpool's cultural links with the USA are probably stronger than anywhere else in the UK, as you would expect, as it was for many centuries the main point of transatlantic travel. The cultural links section is sub divided into:

Entertainment – American stars Halle Berry, Kim Catterall, Mike Myers and Jeff Bridges and Beau Bridges all had one or more Parents who were born in Liverpool and emigrated to America.

Music – The Beatles are the most obvious but there are many others who are less well known.

Art & Literature - Nathaniel Hawthorne, Herman Melville, Washington Irving, Felicia Hemans, Charles Dickens.

Buildings and Institutions – It might be quicker to list the buildings that don't have an American connection.

Entertainment

So lets begin with a look at Liverpool's entertainment links to the United States.

One of the all time great Western films was 'Butch Cassidy and the Sundance Kid' based on two real life characters.

Robert Leroy Parker aka Butch Cassidy was born in Utah, in April 1866 and Harry Alonzo Longbaugh aka The Sundance Kid was born in Pennsylvania.

The Liverpool connection comes from the fact that Mr & Mrs Parker left Liverpool on the ship 'Enoch Train' to begin their long and difficult journey across the Atlantic to New York and then thousands of miles west, largely by foot. A wave of conversions to Mormonism swept through Great Britain in the 19th century, and many British citizens made the arduous voyage across the Atlantic and an equally challenging journey across America to Utah. The families of Maximillian Parker and Ann Gillies made their separate journeys from their homes near Preston, Lancashire to Salt Lake City, the centre of the Mormon faith, and Maximillian and Ann spent their formative years in the Utah wilderness, where they later met each other and later married. On April 13, 1866, the couple welcomed their first of many children, Robert Leroy Parker, who would later become known as 'Butch Cassidy.'

The first major crime attributed to Cassidy is the robbery of the San Miguel Valley Bank in Telluride, on June 24, 1889. He and three cowboys got away with $20,000 by thoroughly casing the joint first. The bandits then made their way over to a choice hideout, Brown's Park, along the Green River at the Utah-Wyoming border. After that, the outlaws held up banks and trains in South Dakota, Wyoming, New Mexico and Nevada, and managed to bring home increasingly large sums of money - like an estimated $70,000 for the holdup of a Rio Grande train near Folsom, New Mexico. But by then, the good old days seemed to be over. By this time, the 'Wild Bunch' had an extensive array of law officers hunting them wherever they went, and Butch had an impressive folio compiled by the Pinkerton National Detective Agency, whose operatives seemed to follow his every move, waiting for a slip-up. It is believed that Butch Cassidy fled the US to Bolivia via a ship which sailed from New York to Liverpool and then on a different vessel from Liverpool to South America where he and Sundance were said to have been killed in a shoot out with Bolivian troops. It is also said that he in fact escaped, from Bolivia and returned to the US under a false identity and lived in New York State secretly until his death.

Mike Myers was born on the 25th of May, 1963 in, Toronto, Canada, His father, Eric, was formerly a cook in the British Army, while his mother, Alice, known as Bunny and formerly in the RAF.

Both originated in Liverpool, and they were married in 1955 emigrating to Canada the next year, They produced three sons - Paul , Peter and finally Mike, all of them holding British passports. Learning the English language from Eric and Bunny, Mike spoke with a Liverpool accent until the age of 6. Mike later starred in the films : Austin Powers, Wayne's World and Shrek amongst many others.

Halle Berry was born on August 14, 1966 in Cleveland, Ohio. Her Mother came from Liverpool in England and her Dad was in the US Air Force. They divorced when she was four years old. When she was 17 years old she won the Miss Teen All-American Pageant. She became a model and after was picked to star in a show called Living Dolls in 1989. In 14 years she starred in eight movies and one weekly TV series in 1989. She starred X-Men in 2000 and X-Men 2 in 2003. In 2001, she starred in the movie Monster's Ball and won an Oscar for Best Actress in 2002 for her performance. She is the first African-American woman to win an Oscar for Best Actress.

Kim Cattrall was born on August 21, 1956 in Liverpool, England. At the age of three months, she emigrated with her father, Dennis, and mother, Shane, to Canada, where a large number of her films have been made. She now lives in the US.

Among her many films and TV shows are - Sex and the City, Police Academy, Porkys, The Bonfire of the Vanities and many more.

Lloyd Bridges was a highly respected actor who made his name as skin diver Mike Nelson in the popular 1950s TV series 'Sea Hunt.' He also starred in the musicals on Broadway, and in his later years he became a comedy sensation through the zany Airplane movies and his occasional turn as Mandelbaum on 'Seinfeld.'

Lloyd died in 1998. Lloyd Bridges's wife, Dorothy, was a formidable presence in her own right. Her friends affectionately refer to her as Dotty, and inside the family, she's affectionately known as The General.

They had two sons who became movie stars in their own right 'My Mom was really something,' Beau says. *'She runs the entire show. Like dad, she was born in California, but her folks were from Liverpool. By the time her father was 14, he had jumped on a sailing ship and run away*

Beau Bridges

Jeff Bridges

from home. By the time he was 21, he had been around the world seven times. He finally settled down in New York, and eventually he became the head of transportation for a Broadway Department Store.

'I've never been to Liverpool but of course I'm very proud of having a grandfather from there because the city has such a wonderful musical heritage.'

Henny Youngman, the undisputed king of the one-liners, whose quip 'Take my wife—please,' defines the Jewish comedic style.

Youngman, whose career was a series of peaks and valleys, ridicule and respect, frequently appeared with a violin (shades of Jack Benny).

But his real trademark was his non-stop series of succinct, acerbic but surprisingly uncontroversial jokes.

He was born to Russian immigrants in Liverpool, England, on January 12, 1906.

His family soon moved to the U.S. and his father made him take violin lessons hoping he would become proficient enough to play professionally. Growing up in Brooklyn's Bay Ridge, Youngman studied printing at Brooklyn Vocational School and did several odd jobs before starting a band .

Here are some Henny Youngman one-liners.

'This guy asked his doctor, 'Will I be able to play the piano after my operation' And the doctor says 'Sure.'
And the guy says, 'Funny, I couldn't do it before.'

'I was so ugly when I was born, the doctor slapped my mother.'

'I know a guy who had his doctor say 'take some weight off, go to a health club.' This man lost 30 pounds in one week! The machine tore his leg off.'

A little Jewish Grandma is at the Florida coast with her little Jewish Grandson. The grandson is playing on the beach when a big wave comes and washes the kid out to sea. The lifeguards swim out, bring him back to shore, the paramedics work on him for a long time, pumping the water out, reviving him. They turn to the Jewish Grandma, and say 'we saved your grandson.' The little Jewish Grandma says 'He had a hat'.

'I asked my wife, 'Where do you want to go for our anniversary' She said, 'Somewhere I have never been!' I told her, 'How about the kitchen?'

'All my wife does is shop - once she was sick for a week, and three stores went broke.'

CHAPTER FIFTEEN

Pop Music

This is about The Beatles and their connections with the United States. Beatlemania exploded in the United States with three national television appearances by the Beatles on The Ed Sullivan Show on 9th February, 16th February and 23rd February, 1964.

The pop-music band became a worldwide phenomenon with worshipful fans and angry denunciations by cultural observers and established performers such as Frank Sinatra, sometimes on grounds of the music (which was thought crude and unmusical) or their appearance (their hair was scandalously long) in effect, the Beatles were in the right place at the right time (with a unique combination of talent and stage presence) to provide an enthusiastic jolt to a saddened nation. In 1964 they held the top five places on the American music industries weekly paper - Billboard's Hot 100, a feat that has never been repeated.

The Beatles performed their last concert before paying fans in Candlestick Park in San Francisco on 29th August, 1966. Twenty-four thousand screaming fans couldn't be wrong.

But what they didn't realize on that late August evening was that the Beatles didn't want to be there, that the band couldn't hear itself enough to sing on-key, and that this would be the last Beatles concert ever.

Strawberry Field was a Salvation Army orphanage in Liverpool, founded in 1936. Strawberry Field had an annual fête, which John Lennon and his aunt Mimi regularly attended.

It closed its doors as a children's home in early January, 2005 and is now a church and prayer centre. The famous gates marking its entrance still stand.

The gates at Strawbery Field, Liverpool

The name of the orphanage became world famous in 1967, with the release of The Beatles single 'Strawberry Fields Forever', written by John Lennon. Lennon grew up near the orphanage and used to play in the wooded area behind the building with his childhood friends.

It was also said that this place inspired Lennon to be a musician.

One of Lennon's childhood treats was the garden party that took place each summer in the grounds of Strawberry Field.

There is another Strawberry Fields situated in America, it is a 2.5 acre landscaped section in New York's Central Park that is dedicated to the memory of musician John Lennon, and named after his song, 'Strawberry Fields Forever.'

Strawberry Fields was inaugurated on Lennon's birthday, 9th October 1985, by his widow Yoko Ono, who had underwritten the project.

Strawbery Fields in Central Park

The entrance to the memorial is located on Central Park West at West 72nd Street, directly across from the Dakota Apartments, where Lennon lived for the latter part of his life and where he was murdered.

The memorial is a triangular piece of land falling away on the two Park sides, whose focal point is a circular pathway mosaic of inlaid stones, a reproduction of a mosaic from Pompeii, made by Italian craftsmen as a gift from the city of Naples.

In the center of the mosaic is a single word, the title of Lennon's famous song: 'Imagine'.

It is not uncommon for the memorial to be covered with flowers, and other belongings left behind by Lennon fans. Every year, on his birthday (October 9th) and on the anniversary of his death (December 8th), people gather to sing songs and pay tribute, staying late into what is often a very cold night in New York.

Sadly, both John Lennon and George Harrison died in America, John in New York and George in Los Angeles.

John Lennon

Born - 9th October 1940
Liverpool, England

Died 8th December 1980
(aged 40)
New York

George Harrison

Born - 25th February 1943
Liverpool, England

Died 29th November 2001
(aged 58)
Los Angeles, California

Jazz

The authors own first Jazz link, is to the Louis Armstrong All-stars concert at the Old Liverpool Stadium behind Exchange Station. This was on Easter Sunday 1956 and due to a ban by the Musicians Union on visiting American Bands, which was lifted in 1956.

Louis's All-stars were the first American Musicians to play in Liverpool since before the War. Nothing since that performance has matched the excitement of that first live concert in Liverpool.

After that American Jazz stars performed in Liverpool regularly, Gerry Mulligan, Count Basie, The Modern Jazz Quartet, and Ella Fitzgerald, Sarah Vaughan at the Odeon in London Road.

Country & Western

Live music has always been an important part of Liverpool culture and, over the years, the city has adopted Celtic, Welsh and American sounds into its musical style. Country music grew from the folk music that was brought to North America by Anglo-Celtic settlers in the 1700s and 1800s.

A commercial offshoot of the folk music of the rural South, country music is an American art form that gained worldwide appeal after World War II. The maritime connection brought a familiarity with the US and by the 1950s Liverpool was a stronghold for imported country and western, soul, jazz and rock and roll. It was this cultural interchange that allowed the city to take the lead in the development of British pop.

Originally known as hillbilly or mountain music, If you went into almost any Liverpool Irish pub in the late 50's, the songs of Hank Williams and Patsy Cline were being performed alongside the traditional jigs and reels.

Fifties Pop

Before the Beatles, Pop music in fifties Liverpool meant appearences at the Liverpool Empire by visiting US singing stars like Frankie Laine and Guy Mitchell, Rosemary Clooney and Joe Stafford, Johnnie Ray and Tony Bennett, Frank Sinatra, Bing Crosby and Al Martino.

Frankie Lane

Guy Mitchell

Rosemary Clooney

Jo Stafford

Johnnie Ray

Tony Bennett

Frank Sinatra

Bing Crosby

Al Martino

CHAPTER SIXTEEN

Literature and Art

Brian Jacques the author of the internationally best selling Redwall novels, was born in Liverpool, in 1939. Brian's Redwall books have become massive best sellers in America. The stories are known as the 'Redwall' series, because they centre around Redwall Abbey. The heroes are peace-loving mice, moles, shrews, squirrels, and their friends who exhibit human characteristics in a medieval setting.

With the publication of his first children's book in 1987, the award winning 'Redwall', Mr Jacques fresh talent has received exceptional praise from reviewers in the United States and England. Newberry Award winner Lloyd Alexander called it 'a fine work, literate, witty, filled with the excitement of genuine storytelling'.

Herman Melville Author of Moby Dick, Billy Budd and many other tales of life at sea in the 19th century. Herman Melville was born on August 1, 1819, in New York City; his father was a prosperous importer,

Herman's roving disposition soon led him to ship as cabin boy in a New York vessel bound for Liverpool. 'Redburn: His First Voyage,' published in 1849, is partly founded on the experiences of this trip. Drawn from Melville's own adolescent experience aboard a merchant ship, 'Redburn' charts the coming-of-age of Wellingborough Redburn, a young innocent who embarks on a crossing to Liverpool together with a roguish crew.

Once in Liverpool, Redburn encounters the squalid conditions of the city and meets Harry Bolton, a bereft and damaged soul, who takes him on a tour of London that includes a scene of rococo decadence unlike anything else in Melville's fiction. In her Introduction, Elizabeth Hardwick writes, 'Redburn is rich in masterful portraits—Redburn is not a document; it is a work of art by the unexpected genius of a sailor, Herman Melville.'

The Princes Dock a dock, on the River Mersey is mentioned in Redburn.

Washington Irving (1783-1859), the first American author to achieve international renown, who created the fictional characters Rip Van Winkle and Ichabod Crane. The critical acceptance and enduring popularity of Irving's tales involving these characters proved the effectiveness of the short story as an American literary form. In 1815 Irving went to Liverpool, England, as a silent partner in his brothers' commercial firm. When, after a series of losses, the business went into bankruptcy in 1818, Irving returned to writing for a living. In England he became the intimate friend of several leading men of letters, including Thomas Campbell, Sir Walter Scott, and Thomas Moore.

Nathaniel Hawthorne

(Born: 4th July 1804 Birthplace: Salem, Massachusetts Died: 19th May 1864) Best known as, the author of 'The Scarlet Letter'. One of the great American authors of the 19th century, Nathaniel Hawthorne grew up in New England and published his first novel, 'Fanshawe', in 1828. Though he went on to help lay the foundations of the American short story, Hawthorne is more widely known for his novels 'The Scarlet Letter' (1850) and 'The House of Seven Gables' (1851). Mr Hawthorne who lodged at 186 Duke Street was appointed American Consul to Liverpool, serving from 1853 to 1857.

Since the publication of 'The Scarlet Letter' in 1850, Nathaniel Hawthorne has been recognized as one of America's most important writers, both a 'romancer' who probed inner mysteries and a 'realist' who assessed the American character and experience. *'Happiness is as a butterfly which when pursued is always beyond our grasp, but which if you will sit down quietly may alight upon you'* - Nathaniel Hawthorne

Felicia Hemans (1793 - 1835)

Born at 118 Duke Street Liverpool, later became one of the best-selling poets of her day. Felicia was the most widely read female poet of the English-speaking world throughout the nineteenth century and into the early twentieth.

During her lifetime, she published 20 volumes of poetry and placed nearly 400 poems in magazines and annuals.

She was reviewed favourably in her lifetime by the major periodicals and was spoken of in the same breath as Wordsworth, Byron, Shelley and Keats. After her death in 1835, scores of selected and collected editions appeared until the rise of modernism.

Schoolchildren in the U. S. are still being taught the classic poem by Felicia Hemens 'The Landing of the Pilgrim Fathers in New England'.

Mark Twain (1835-1910)

The noted American author visited Liverpool on a number of occasions.

He wrote the well known books - 'Adventures of Tom Sawyer' and 'Huckleberry Finn'.

During a visit to Liverpool in 1873, as part of a European lecture tour, the noted American author Mark Twain stayed at the Washington Hotel in Lime Street and was later entertained at a special Lord Mayors banquet at the Town hall.

He wrote in a letter home.

Original Adelphi Hotel

'We arrived in Liverpool an hour ago very tired, and have halted at this hotel (The Washington in Lime Street - by the advice of misguided friends)—and if my instinct and experience are worth anything, it is the very worst hotel on earth, without any exception.

We shall move to another hotel (He moved further down Lime Street to the Adelphi Hotel) early in the morning to spend to-morrow. Then we sail from Liverpool for America the next day in the 'Gallic.'

Mark Twain later wrote a poem about old age in which he made reference to Liverpool.

To the Old People

The Joy of Life, that streaming through their Veins
Tumultuous swept, falls slack—and wanes
The Glory in the Eye—and one by one
Life's Pleasures perish and make place for Pains.
Whether one hides in some secluded Nook—
Whether at Liverpool or Sandy Hook—
Some for the Honours of Old Age, and some
Long for its Respite from the Hum
And Clash of sordid Strife—O Fools,
The Past should teach them what's to Come:

Later in an article describing the silver mining boom of the 1890s in Nevada he mentioned Liverpool again in the following extract

Roughing It - by Mark Twain.

'They transported the ore concentrated to Europe. The conveyance from Star City (its locality) to Virginia City will cost 70 dollars per ton; from Virginia to San Francisco, 40 dollars per ton; from thence to Liverpool, its destination, ten dollars per ton.

Their idea is that its conglomerate metals will reimburse them their cost of original extraction, the price of transportation, and the expense of reduction, and that then a ton of the raw ore will net them 1200 dollars'.

ART

A travelling exhibition currently on view in the A. A. Low Building of the South Street Seaport Museum in New York City presents some thirty ship portraits executed during the nineteenth century. Entitled Across the Western Ocean: American Ships by Liverpool Painters.

In 1818 a group of enterprising New Yorkers founded the Black Ball Line, which operated a scheduled packet service between Liverpool and New York. The idea of a timetable was both innovative and immediately successful, since the confirmed pickup and delivery of freight, passengers, mail, and specie gave the shipping line a monopoly on the Atlantic.

A number of other firms were founded shortly afterward, and in less than a decade these companies dominated trade between England and America.

Passengers, and the trade of American raw materials and agricultural products for British manufactured goods, ensured hefty profits. For a variety of reasons the attempts of Boston, Philadelphia, and Baltimore to supplant New York City's maritime fleet dominating the Liverpool trade were not successful.

As American trade with Europe flourished following the War of 1812, Liverpool became the largest port in England. American ship-owners, seamen, and shipbuilders commissioned artists to paint their vessels' portraits, and soon a school of Liverpool artists was fulfilling these commissions.

Liverpool's location at the terminus of railroad and canal systems that connected it to the Midlands - England's industrial center - made it an ideal port. It grew so quickly that by 1840 there was dock space for more than one thousand ships at a time. By 1850 nearly one-quarter of the ships that put into port there were American-owned. In the same period more than twenty thousand European and British emigrants were boarding outbound ships each month.

The Liverpool ship portraitists included some professionals, but most were also engaged as shipbuilders, house painters, plumbers, or tobacconists, among other occupations, who accepted commissions for ship portraits to supplement their income.

Pride in their vessels occasioned owners to demand a high degree of accuracy, and among the most widely sought artists were those familiar with the rigging of a ship and other technicalities. The Liverpool artists were in demand until England's paddle steamers came to dominate the seas in the 1850s and the Civil War disrupted, and ultimately ended, American shipping interests abroad.

Perhaps the best known of the Liverpool artists was Robert Salmon (1775-c. 1845), who had exhibited at London's Royal Academy before coming to Liverpool. There he painted about one hundred works between 1806 and 1811, and then returned to paint some eighty more between about 1822 and 1825. Eventually Salmon emigrated to Boston, where he excelled in painting harbour views and marine subjects.

Among the lesser-known but talented artists whose work is represented in the exhibition is John Jenkinson (w. 1790-1821), whose paintings are accomplished enough to have been hitherto confused with Salmon's.

Miles Walters (1773-1855) was born in North Devon, England, and apprenticed to a shipwright before moving to London to establish himself as a painter, frame maker, and gilder. His arrival in Liverpool in 1827 (the date inscribed on his first-known Liverpool painting) was fortuitous because Jenkinson was dead and Salmon was in America, leaving a niche for a skilled artist like Walters.

His son, Samuel (1811-1882), was also a marine artist of note and the family dominated this field for some time.

Liverpool University Art Gallery

John James Audubon (1785-1851) was an American nineteenth century wildlife artist and naturalist. He travelled the American wilderness identifying, studying and drawing hundreds of species of birds and mammals. Audubon gave himself the title of the 'American Woodsman' and became a national icon.

The University of Liverpool Art Collections holds the largest collection of original oil paintings by Audubon outside America.

On 21 July 1826 John James Audubon arrived at the port of Liverpool. The following day Audubon received an invitation to dine at 87 Duke Street with William Roscoe, who amongst other things was an art collector and a founder of the Liverpool Royal Institution.

It was agreed that Audubon should exhibit his paintings at the Royal Institution.

Audubon wanted to repay the kindness he had received in Liverpool and decided to do this by drawing or painting parting gifts.

For the Royal Institution he chose to paint a large oil version of his 'Wild Turkey Cock'. Audubon presented the gift with the following letter:

'Gentlemen,

I take the liberty of offering you with a painting of the Wild American Turkey Cock. Please accept it – it is alas a poor return for the many kind attentions received by me from you all. Permit me at the same time to consider myself, Gentlemen,

Yours Most Respectfully,

John J Audubon. Liverpool August. 20th 1826'

CHAPTER SEVENTEEN

Buildings and Institutions

Evered Avenue Library

T here are numerous buildings and institutions in Liverpool which have American associations – here below are some lesser known examples.

Evered Avenue Library in Rice Lane, Walton, Liverpool, was one of many libraries in Britain and throughout the USA, endowed by the Andrew Carnegie Trust.

Andrew Carnegie was born in Dunfermline, Scotland, on November 25, 1835. The son of a weaver, he came with his family to the United States in 1848 and settled in Allegheny, Pennsylvania. At age 13 Carnegie went to work as a bobbin boy in a cotton mill.

He then moved rapidly through a succession of jobs with Western Union and the Pennsylvania Railroad. In 1865, he resigned to establish his own business enterprises and eventually organized the Carnegie Steel Company, which launched the steel industry in Pittsburgh. At an early age he sold the company to J. P. Morgan for $480 million and devoted the rest of his life to his philanthropic activities.

Many persons of wealth have contributed to charity, but Carnegie was perhaps the first to state publicly that the rich have

Andrew Carnegie

a moral obligation to give away their fortunes. In 1889 he wrote 'The Gospel of Wealth', in which he asserted that all personal wealth beyond that required to supply the needs of one's family should be regarded as a trust fund to be administered for the benefit of the community.

One of Carnegie's lifelong interests was the establishment of free public libraries to make available to everyone a means of self-education. During his lifetime, Carnegie gave away over $350 million. He died in Lenox, Massachusetts, on August 11, 1919.

Mersey Mission to Seamen

Mersey Mission to Seamen

The Reverend James Fell was originally the Chaplain at the Mersey Mission to Seamen based in Hanover Street,Liverpool, and later travelled to San Francisco shortly after the Gold Rush.

At that time San Francisco was one of the wildest places on earth and the most lawless part of it was the notorious Barbary Coast area on what is now called Fisherman's Wharf.

It was here in 1881 the Rev. James Fell started the Sailor's Institute in San Francisco.

The Reverend Fell, who carried a six-shooter was said to have cleared the bars and brothels single handed within ten years.

Rev. James Fell

He wrote an excellent book about the dangers facing British Seamen in San Francisco 'British Merchant Seamen In San Francisco - 1892 - 1896.

San Francisco Harbour

(*There is an appendix with extracts from it at the rear of this book)

In Chapter Seven he writes 'Seamen who desert their ship sacrifice all the wages they may have earned on the voyage. And come ashore penniless.

Why do the Crimps try to induce men to desert their ships-they cannot rob them as they have nothing to take.

The answer is that he is a most valuable piece of merchandise and great profits often accrue out of his desertion.

It is generally speaking a very bad thing for a sailor to desert his ship in San Francisco. Some few hit upon a good job, but very few. A certain number would do a little wandering in California, getting an odd job here and there on a ranch, or in the Goldfields then make their way back to San Francisco to sign up for another voyage on another ship - having lost all their wages.'

The International Maritime centre in Oakland, California has described the work of James Fell in a recent article:

'In 1881, English clergyman James Fell founded the Sailors Institute in San Francisco. A Gold Rush-era predecessor preached aboard ships, but the Reverend Fell was the first to provide mariners with permanent quarters for lodging and recreation. The notorious 'Barbary Coast', Fell observed, was 'a special dread to mothers of young square-rigger sailors.' Tirelessly he championed 'a safe haven to keep them from the terrible temptations of a seaport town, a place to escape the wiles of the whole army of men and women who make their livelihood by preying on them when they land.'

He envisioned *'a place where the sailor may find every comfort and lodging and all manner of games, and papers, where he may write his letters and smoke his pipe on the weekday evenings, and make himself thoroughly at home, and be able to enjoy concerts and music once or twice a week.'*

Fell secured funds to build the Institute from the Missions Society of the Anglican Church, local merchants and shippers. An admirer wrote that he worked *'single handedly, in the teeth of bitter opposition and not infrequently murderous threats.'*

One month after the Institute opened at 33 Stuart Street, Fell reported that 1,000 ships officers, apprentices and seamen had visited, and many of them lodged there. Twenty-five years later, the building was destroyed in the San Francisco earthquake and fire. 'Scarcely before the ashes were cold,' however, Fell toured the site with the bishop of the just-created Episcopal Diocese of California. The new facility opened less than a year later at 58 Clay Street. The Rev Fell returned to Liverpool (he believed there might be some more bad guys there) and to the Mersey Mission to Seamen.

He later retired and went to live in the Lake District.

Albion House – White Star Line

Albion House, James Street, Liverpool. It was built for the Ismay, Imrie and Company shipping company, which later became the White Star Line. The significance of Albion House (formerly the White Star headquarters) to the Titanic is that the disaster was announced to the wives and families of the crew from the safety of the first floor balcony.

Bruce Ismay, the chairman of the White Star line, lived in Waterloo and White Star liners would sound their sirens as they went past his house. Ismay was later vilified for saving himself when the Titanic went down.

At the time of the Titanic disaster, White Star had been taken over by J P Morgan, the American financial magnate. Later on, it was to be merged with Cunard.

The Lyceum

This gentlemen's club, library and reading room at the corner of Bold Street, was founded in 1799 by a group which included William Roscoe.

When American author Herman Melville (Moby Dick) visited Liverpool in 1841 as a young sailor of 19 he wished to visit the Lyceum as his father, a prosperous American businessman, had 30 years before.

The Lyceum also became home to Liverpool's subscription library, founded in 1757. This is believed to have been the first circulating or lending library in Europe.

The Athenaeum

The Athenaeum situated between Church Street and the Bluecoat Chambers is a haven in the heart of Liverpool that offers a distinguished setting and an atmosphere unrivalled in the city of Liverpool. It was founded in 1797 to provide a meeting place where ideas and information could be exchanged.

The Neo-classical building was designed by architect

Thomas Harrison of Chester and was built between 1800–1802. The club's founders, members of the Liverpool Literary and Philosophical Society – who included several of Liverpool's Slavery abolitionists (notably William Roscoe) – wanted to establish an alternative meeting place to the often rowdy merchants' coffee houses.

In 1848, the American author Washington Irvine wrote in his sketchbook, *'One of the first places to which a stranger is taken in Liverpool is the Athenaeum; it contains a good library and a spacious reading room and is the great literary resource of the place.'*

The Boston Athenaeum, one of the oldest and most distinguished independent libraries in the United States, was founded in 1807 by members of the Anthology Society,

Their purpose was to form *'an establishment similar to that of the Athenaeum and Lyceum of Liverpool in Great Britain; combining the advantages of a public library [and] containing the great works of learning and science in all languages.'*

William Brown Street Library

William Brown 1884 – 1864 born in Antrim Ireland, William aged 16 set sail for America with his father and mother. The family settled in Baltimore where his father continued in the linen trade.

In 1809, with the firm outgrowing local trade, William was sent back to the UK, to establish a branch in Liverpool.

Following the death of his father, the business, under the control of himself and his three brothers, continued to expand: William was based in Liverpool, John in Philadelphia, George in Baltimore, and James in New York.

William Brown will be best remembered in Liverpool for the magnificent gift he bestowed on his adopted town, namely the Liverpool Public Library and Museum whose construction costs (reported to be £40,000) he paid for.

Subsequently, the corporation named the library building and the street where they stand after Brown. William Brown died at his home, Richmond Hill, Liverpool, on 3rd March 1864.

The Adelphi Hotel

The first Adelphi Hotel on the present site was opened in 1826 by owner James Radley. It soon became the most popular hotel in the city, and gained a reputation throughout Britain and Europe.

In 1912, another great hotelier, Arthur Towle, acquired and rebuilt the Adelphi. Today's building still reflects his care and ambition to make it one of the most luxurious in Europe, with solid marble walls in many of the bedrooms, a fine indoor heated swimming pool, sauna and full central heating.

The Sefton Suite is in fact a replica of the First Class Smoking Lounge on the ill fated 'Titanic'.

The following years saw a flourishing trade, with the hotel as Liverpool's arrival and departure point for passengers on the great liners to America and beyond.

Many famous people and visiting movie stars have stayed in both the present and the previous Adelphi Hotel, including American cowboy film star Roy Rogers and his horse 'Trigger', who made a grand entrance from the mezzanine floor to the main lounge.

US President Jefferson Davis stayed here in 1868, as well as American author Mark Twain.

The Cunard Building

The Cunard building was the centre of Britain's cruise ship industry for many years, a land based reflection of the glory and wealth of cruise liners.

Constructed between 1914 and 1918 its design is influenced by grand Italian palaces and reflects the Greek neo-classical revival. Owned by American Samuel Cunard, who sent the first mail boats across the Atlantic, the building has American Eagles looking down on each corner.

Cunard later merged with White Star owners of the 'Titanic', some of the company's famous ships included the 'Mauritania', 'Queen Elizabeth', and the 'Queen Mary'.

Cruise liners were once a common sight on the River Mersey, millions of people passed through Liverpool on their way to or from North America.

Passengers included immigrants sailing to a new life, tourists and celebrities, as before the advent of air travel the only way to cross the 3,140 miles of ocean to New York was by liner.

Passengers travelling with Cunard would arrive at the Cunard Building to deposit luggage, change money and make last minute arrangements.

The basement of the building housed the luggage to be stowed in the hold, within the building there is an ornate corridor with a black and white marble floor linking Brunswick Street and Water Street.

The first class passenger waiting room is on the river side of the building and has all the luxury and fittings that would provide a foretaste of the elegance of life aboard ship.

Cruise Liners were like a small town with a large staff and a long list of requirements, Cunard Liners mainly used Huskisson Dock until the 1960s. Prior to 1919 North Atlantic liners used coal to fuel their engines, the 'Olympic' was the first ship to switch to oil. Loading of coal onto the great liner 'Mauritania' needed 500 railway wagons, took 24 hours and was a messy business, all of the ships furniture had to be covered with sheets, stewards and cleaners then had a day to scrub paintwork clean.

When a liner arrived for an overhaul it would take four weeks and employ 2000 people to clean and paint every last nook and cranny of the ship.

The liners provided employment for armies of people in Liverpool, each time one arrived as the last passengers left down the gang plank heading the other way was a procession of painters, cleaners, plumbers and a variety of other trades people who would go onboard to prepare the ship for her next voyage.

In the 1900s, there were approximately 300 laundries in the city, providing the thousands of clean sheets, towels and napkins needed for a voyage.

Cunard's New York building seen here on the left, is a much more modest affair than the Liverpool building and reflects Cunard's emphasis on its American operations as having a more subsidiary role in their hierarchy.

CHAPTER EIGHTEEN

Trade & Commerce

Liverpool's trade with North America (USA & Canada) began in the 1660s bringing back mainly tobacco and sugar.

As the continent developed and ships became larger and faster, trade grew and Liverpool exported manufactured items such as cloth and pottery, and imported raw materials and foodstuffs.

The best known examples of Liverpool's transatlantic trade would be shipping, cotton, slave trade, emigration and the transatlantic passenger trade.

Of these only shipping is still active which serves to export products stored in containers from all over the UK.

In the 21st century almost all trading from Liverpool to the USA is from the giant container base at Seaforth Docks. But we will begin with the shameful story of Liverpool's part in the infamous slave trade.

Slave Trade

The slave triangle is a depressing piece of world history involving a variety of culprits in England, France, Spain, Portugal, African chiefs and Arab traders from the Arab countries of the middle east. The victims were poor Africans - men, women, and children.

The first part of the triangle was called the outer passage when Europeans sailed to Africa where prisoners were sold to European slavers in return for cheap manufactured goods, textiles and alcohol.

The slaves were then transported across the Atlantic in the second part of the  triangle (called The Middle Passage) and sold to work on plantations growing sugar, cotton, tobacco and many other crops. The final leg of the slave triangle was the Return Passage when goods like cotton, sugar and rum were brought back from America to Britain and other countries in Europe.

Liverpool played a major role in the transportation of these poor victims of greed and exploitation, which constituted the second or middle part of the triangle of evil.

An estimated 15 million Africans were transported as slaves to the Americas between 1540 and 1850. Ships from Liverpool accounted for more than 40% of the European slave trade.

The town and its inhabitants derived great wealth from the trade. It laid the foundations for the town's growth.

It is no exaggeration to say that the grand buildings which grace Liverpool's waterfront and inner heart today were built with the blood money of slavery.

The Wilberforce Lecture by the Bishop of Liverpool, the Rt. Rev. James Jones: Slavery and Racism – 21 March 2007 said,

'*The Establishment countenanced both slavery and the trade fearing that abolition would threaten the British Empire with economic ruin. The Bishops, with the notable exception of the Bishop of Chester, Reilly Porteus, who later went on to become 'Bishop of London' sided with the Establishment. Adam Hochschild in his book 'Bury the Chains' tells of a plantation in the West Indies which was owned by the Society for the Propagation of the Gospel in Foreign Parts, whose governing board included the Regius Professors of Divinity at Oxford and Cambridge and the Archbishop of Canterbury. The estate's brand, burned onto the chests of slaves with a red-hot iron, was SOCIETY. The clerics on the society's board noticed the plantation's high death rate, but made no move to change how it operated. 'I have long wondered & lamented,' wrote the Archbishop of Canterbury to a fellow bishop in 1760, 'that the Negroes in our plantations decrease, & new supplies become necessary continually. Surely this proceeds from defect, both of humanity, & even of good policy. But we must take things as they are at present.'*

So much for the prophetic moral vision of the Church of England! And even the evangelicals who eventually emerged as a driving force of the abolition movement were possessed of a personal piety which sought principally the conversion of others so that slave owning converts in the Colonies would lead more upright lives and their converted slaves would become more industrious'

There was however some opposition from sections of the public in Liverpool, mainly from 'The Liverpool Anti-Slavery Committee' led by the Liverpool Quaker John Cropper.

In 1824 a letter was sent on behalf of the committee and addressed to 'The People of North America' deploring the situation and calling for an end to all forms of slavery in the US.

'Deep and solemn convictions compel us to thus address you. We feel that slavery, wherever it exists, involves an aggravated violation of man's rights and Gods laws; that it is evil both to the enslaved and to the enslaver; that it is a stain on the national honour, and a blot on its religious character, and that in its extinction your duty and interests are equally combined.'

Cotton Trade

Liverpool has been importing cotton from the southern states of the USA since 1709, it has been shaped by the many people and places involved in the cotton trade.

Liverpool is a cosmopolitan city and the global nature of the cotton trade contributed to this. There were brokers from all over the world based here in the 19th century, including Germany, Prussia, Russia, Greece, the USA and India.

Many of Liverpool's famous names were made rich from cotton, including the Rathbones and the Holts. Wealthy cotton merchants and brokers who lived in Liverpool's finest houses.

The first American cotton was unloaded in Liverpool in 1784. There were only eight bags. Less than 40 years later, half a million bales were arriving each year from America.

Liverpool and Lancashire felt the direct consequences of the Civil War as the Northern navy blockaded the Southern ports. Cotton imports to Liverpool were halted, Liverpool's trade was disrupted and even more so at the Lancashire mills where the owners laid off many thousands of workers.

By November 1862, three fifths of the labour force, 331,000 men and women were idle. Many operatives, their savings exhausted, were forced to apply for charitable handouts or for relief from the despised poor law system.

Such hardships, however, they endured calmly because they believed in the noble cause for which Lincoln was fighting, the freeing of the slaves of the southern plantation owners.

Liverpool Cotton Exchange became the greatest market in the world for the buying and selling of cotton.

In the second half of the nineteenth century much of the initiative in marketing cotton round the globe shifted from Liverpool and London to the American east coast ports.

American merchants were much closer to the cotton plantations and unfettered by the rigid demarcations that had matured in Lancashire.

Eventually the American merchants undermined the Liverpool system by bypassing the traditional buying agencies in the plantation states and the selling agencies in Europe, and began supplying the mills directly.

The cotton merchants and brokers traditionally met on Exchange Flags to do their buying and selling.

In 1808, a Cotton Exchange Building opened, but while cotton brokers took offices there, they preferred to conduct their business in the open square.

Exchange Flags, Liverpool

Cotton traders in Exchange Flags

During the 19th century, American plantation owners in their top hats and frock coats, sold their produce in the open air on Exchange Flags behind Liverpool Town Hall.

The cotton market continued to meet out of doors until the 1800s.

The Flags were a place to meet and swap information about the cotton market.

A purpose-built Cotton Exchange was commissioned and completed in 1906.

This was a state of the art building, with telephones and direct cables to the New York, Bremen and Bombay cotton exchanges.

New technologies like the telegraph and telephone played a major part in moving the cotton men indoors.

Liverpool continued to act as a central clearing house and market for USA raw cotton by importing all supplies and then re-exporting to other countries that raw cotton not required by the English market.

Today the Cotton Trade in Liverpool is now confined to international brokerage.

Transatlantic Shipping

Liverpool's American shipping links have inevitably evolved over many centuries and been driven by changing patterns of commerce, emigration, and travel.

Until the middle of the twentieth century the only way to cross the Atlantic was by ship, and one of the main UK departure ports was Liverpool.

Two of the greatest Atlantic shipping lines, Cunard and White Star, were based in the city. At the height of their popularity the lives of thousands of people on Merseyside were linked with the Atlantic liners, as passengers, crew, employees and suppliers. A liner at sea was a self-contained world.

Liverpool as seen from Birkenhead

Henry Tingle Wilde,
Titanic's Chief Officer

Cunard had its beginnings in 1838 when Canadian shipping magnate Samuel Cunard, along with engineer Robert Napier, and businessmen James Donaldson, George Burns, and David MacIver formed the British and North American Royal Mail Steam Packet Company.

The company successfully bid on the rights to run a transatlantic shipping company between England and America. Later, it would change its name to Cunard Steamships Limited becoming the greatest name in ocean travel in history.

In 1840 the company's first steamship, the 'Britannia', sailed from Liverpool to Boston marking the beginning of regular passenger and cargo service. Cunard faced many competitors from Britain, the United States and Germany but survived them all. This was mainly due to a great focus on safety.

Cunard ships were usually not the largest or the fastest but they were the most reliable and the safest.

RMS Titanic

One of the great stories of the 'Titanic' is called The Two Gold Watches.

Thomas & Ada Hewitt

These watches belonged to Thomas & Ada Hewitt. They lived in 94, Devonfield Road in the Orrell Park area of Liverpool. The watches were gifts to each other on their wedding day in 1902.

You may be able to see that Ada is wearing hers on her shirt in this photo.

The back of Tom's watch was engraved with, 'From Ada to Tom 16-9-02'.

Mr Hewitt was a steward with the Cunard Line.

As part of his journey from his home in Liverpool to join his ship he would take the train from Orrell Park into Liverpool city centre, each time he was taken to the station by Ada and their son and daughter. On his last train journey from Orrell Park station, on his way to Southampton to meet up with Titanic, he waved to his family until they were out of sight After the disaster, Ada wondered whether he had had a premonition as it was the only time he had waved to them like that – maybe he did.

When 'Titanic' sank, after hitting an iceberg at 11:40pm on 14th April 1912, Tom was one of over 1500 people who lost their lives.

Tom Hewitt's body was recovered, but Ada was now a widow with two children to raise and could not afford to have him shipped back to Liverpool. He is believed to be buried in Halifax, Nova Scotia (on the east coast of Canada). It is said that Thomas managed to pass his watch to a stewardess who was leaving Titanic. She was one of the rescued and was able to hand the watch to Cunard officials in New York.

It was later returned it to Ada and their two children in Devonfield Road Liverpool.

The watch is now on display at the Maritime Museum Liverpool.

The prosperous company eventually absorbed Canadian Northern Steamships Limited as well as Cunard's principal competition, the White Star Line, owners of the ill-fated 'RMS Titanic'.

For more than a century and a half, the Cunard Line dominated the Atlantic passenger trade and was one of the world's most important companies.

The Cunard Yanks

One of the effects of the trans- Atlantic shipping and particularly Cunard's huge passenger trade, was the employment of large sections of the population of Merseyside in providing the crews for these liners.

These young men became the trend-setters of their day having access to the very latest in young men's clothing, pop music, and dance crazes with American bought midnight blue tonic mohair suits, slip-on shoes, button-down or tab-collar shirts and 'jazzy' ties. Liverpool has been a cosmopolitan city for centuries, and because it faced the Atlantic, literally and metaphorically, was always the British city closest to the United States.

The so-called 'Cunard Yankees' who worked the liners, were not the first to import American mass culture but to the youth of Liverpool in the drab, gray streets and the florescent dance halls, like 'The Grafton', 'The Locarno', and 'The Rialto', these young seafarers were the princes of style and fashion.

The former seamen, now in their late sixties and seventies, are still cultural icons even now, having just released (2007) a successful movie about their life and times.

The New York-Liverpool connection

A look at Liverpool's American connections by the French writer Professor François Poirier - Université Paris.

'In many ways, this culture of a privileged relationship to an America epitomized by New York was revived by the two world wars, as it is through Liverpool that many things American entered Britain: the sinking of the Lusitania in 1915, with mostly American passengers, but a Liverpool ship with a Liverpool crew, triggered anti-German riots on Merseyside.

When the US entered the war seriously, most of the shipping of troops and equipment came from New York to Liverpool, and the same was true on a larger scale during the Second World War, when the Irish sea proved comparatively safer than the English Channel, and the Western Approaches High Command had its headquarters and bunker in Liverpool.

Liverpool became, after London, the place where the GIs, 'overpaid, oversexed and over here', ★ could find some amusement, in the rough and tumble of a major international sea port, in the cosmopolitan whorehouses, and in the local pubs already catering for a global market — amusements very similar to those of the sailing days, if one is to believe prudish Herman Melville.

When the war was over, many returned to America with a newly acquired English wife, with a greater proportion of Liverpudlians among them than demographic statistics would allow.

Other Liverpool lassies were abandoned, sometimes with child, but soon found another ground to conquer with the US base of Burtonwood near Liverpool — and by the way, at the time of the Beatles' teens, this was a readier source of American music than the erratic life of anarchistic seafarers'

Extract from a lecture given by Professor Poirier.

Authors Note: * An unknown American responded to this description of their GIs by describing the British as ' Underpaid, Undersexed, and Under us'

Liverpool sailing ships now berthed in the United States

SS Wavertree was built in England in 1885 for R.W. Leyland & Company of Liverpool, one of the last large sailing ships built of wrought iron, she is the largest vessel of its type afloat.

'Wavertree' was first employed to carry jute, used in making rope and burlap bags, between eastern India (now Bangladesh) and Scotland.

When less then two years old she entered the tramp trades, taking cargoes anywhere in the world she could find them.

After sailing for a quarter century, she limped into the Falkland Islands in December 1910, having been dismasted off Cape Horn. Rather then re-rigging her, her owners sold her for use as a floating warehouse at Punta Arenas, Chile.

She was converted into a sand barge at Buenos Aires, Argentina in 1947, and acquired by the South Street Seaport Museum in 1968.

'SS Wavertree' this renovated American landmark is right on Lower Manhattan's historic waterfront at Pier 17, South Street, New York, and is currently undergoing restoration to her appearance as a sailing vessel.

Star of India was built in Ramsey, Isle of Man by Gibson McDonald and Arnold in 1863 as 'Euterpe', a full-rigged iron windjammer ship .

She was fitted out at a Liverpool yard and put into service for her owners – Wakefield Nash & Company of Liverpool.

Named after Euterpe, the muse of music, she was a full-rigged ship (a ship that has 3 masts and square sails on all 3 masts), for the Indian jute trade. 'Euterpe's' career had a rough beginning. She sailed for Calcutta from Liverpool on January 9, 1864, under the command of Captain William John Storry. A collision with an unlighted, hit-and-run Spanish brig off the coast of Wales carried away the jib-boom and damaged other rigging. The crew became mutinous, refusing to continue, and she returned to Anglesey for repair; 17 of the crew were confined to the Beaumaris Gaol, and given a sentence of hard labour.

After a full career sailing from Great Britain to India then to New Zealand, she became a salmon hauler on the Alaska to California route.

After retirement, she was restored and is now a seaworthy museum ship ported in San Diego, California.

The ship is both a California and National Historic Landmark, and the latter designation places it on the American National Register of Historic Places.

21st Century Maritime Connections

In the 21st century almost all trading from Liverpool to the USA is from the giant container base at Seaforth Docks.

Today, it handles more container trade with the United States of America and Canada than any other port in the land. Other developments in the global container market have opened up a whole range of new routes for shippers moving their goods through the Seaforth Terminal, adding further benefits to a facility already acknowledged as Britain's most efficient container gateway.

The Mersey Docks and Harbour Company's decision to look at developing a river container terminal capable of handling the new generation of larger post Panamax vessels reflects the new dawn Liverpool is facing.

Other elements of the Port's diverse range of cargoes have added further optimism to the Port's prospects with new trades and rising volumes which totalled a record 32,226,000 tonnes in 2004.

But an increasingly significant influence upon Liverpool's success is the Port's geographic location as the gateway to the second richest cargo hinterland in the country and its ease of access by road and rail.

CHAPTER NINETEEN

Conclusions

The connections between Liverpool and the United States of America are overwhelmingly maritime and began with the first tentative journeys across the Atlantic Ocean to the New World.

These initial links were from east to west, from Europe to the 'New World', as it was called then.

Christopher Columbus: 1451 - 1506, Spanish navigator and colonialist is credited as the first European to discover the Americas in 1492, although a multitude of other unsubstantiated claims have also been made.

Sir Walter Raleigh. 1552 - 1618, was responsible for establishing the first English colony in the 'New World', on June 4, 1584, at Roanoke Island in present-day North Carolina.

The thirteen British colonies in North America were founded between 1607 (Virginia), and 1732 (Georgia). They subsequently constituted the first 13 states of the United States of America.

Liverpool's American history really came after this period, as most transatlantic voyages originated from small ports in the South West of England.

Liverpool's trade with North America began in the 1660s (about 40 years before the slave trade began).

The new settlers in Virginia and Maryland (in America), provided an important and ready market for household goods, farm supplies and clothing. The import of tobacco and sugar from these areas soon became vital to Liverpool's trade.

While there is evidence that a couple of ships brought back one or two cargoes of sugar to Liverpool in 1665, it was not until the creation of sugar refineries in the town, around 1673, that imports began to increase significantly, initially bringing back tobacco and sugar.

By the 1660s Liverpool ships were making direct voyages to Virginia for tobacco. Sugar and tobacco imports began to increase rapidly at the beginning of the 18th century.

As the continent developed, and ships became larger and faster, trade grew. Liverpool began exporting manufactured items such as cloth and pottery, and imported raw materials and foodstuffs.

The development of English colonies in North America and the West Indies provided ready markets for British made goods.

Liverpool was exporting and importing a wide variety of goods by the 17th century. Sugar and tobacco imports had become central to the Liverpool economy by the 18th century at which time local merchants began to take an active role in the slave trade.

As the century progressed, the trade in sugar, tobacco and slaves increased at the same time.

Liverpool's development into Britain's premier trading port was inexorably linked with emergence of the United States as a rapidly developing nation after Independence.

'Liverpool had such pre-eminence in maritime trade between the two continents that shortly after the Californian Gold Rush, a group of merchants on the east coast of America shipped their goods from the port of New York, across the Atlantic to Liverpool, and then from Liverpool around Cape Horn to San Francisco.

The merchandise arrived on the west coast of California at half the rate being charged by the railroad to bring it from New York to San Francisco'.

Irving Stone – Men to Match My Mountains.

This happened because of the exorbitant freight costs being charged by the Union Pacific Railroad Company to carry the goods over 3000 miles by rail to San Francisco from the East Coast.

Liverpool's role as the premier port of embarkation to the New World rapidly increased during the year 1846 as people fled from the famine in Ireland. This massive exodus was followed by smaller but significant ethnic groups from all over Europe.

It is estimated that over nine million people travelled out to America from the Port of Liverpool. The advent of steam driven ships brought the journey time across the ocean down to less than ten days.

Soon greatly increased safety, and the shorter crossing time of travelling across the Atlantic, gave birth to a prosperous new industry, Transatlantic travel, and Liverpool became its natural home.

At it's peak during the second world war, the port had over thirteen miles of docks, with huge brick warehouses, the biggest in the world, built to hold the cargoes of every description which were coming to, and going from, the port.

The two world wars of the twentieth century greatly increased the number of linkages between Liverpool and America.

Massive amounts of supplies and troops arrived in Liverpool from America to sustain both the first and second world wars.

Liverpool's historical connections with the United States began over three hundred years ago with it's evolution into a pre-eminent Transatlantic Port, and then that multitude of historical events and connections with America, began to fade proportionately, as those shipping links gradually began to decline.

Since the end of the war in 1945, Liverpool's maritime industry began to decline.

This has been largely due to dramatic global economic changes, and trade patterns, rather than as the national media would have us believe, poor industrial relations and high local labour costs.

This evidence can clearly be seen in the American east coast ports like Boston, New York, Philadelphia and Baltimore, where the decline in transatlantic shipping has devastated the local economies, and which have all had to reinvent themselves during the last 25 years.

The biggest factor in the decline of Liverpool's maritime industry has been the ending of the Transatlantic passenger trade, and its replacement by international air travel.

A massive trade in cargoes of every description still exists of course, but now it goes in containers from the huge container base at Seaforth Docks.

I was reminded of the effects of those profound changes recently as I watched an endless stream of vehicles carrying their load of containers to and from the docks.

I realised that in fact that there were almost no human contacts involved in the

21st century in the movement of such great quantities of goods, from their original shipment point, to their final destinations across the ocean.

All of those economic factors have brought about the end of an era, and an end to the potential for the creation of any further links and connection of the kind described in this book, between Liverpool and the United States.

Today many of those events from the past, described in this book, have all but disappeared from the pages of Liverpool's history, and that is one of the reasons for this book.

Let us end this long journey through Liverpool's Maritime history on a positive note.

As the year of European Capital of Culture 2008 approaches and a new cruise liner terminal on the River Mersey is completed, an exciting new chapter in Liverpool's maritime history is about to begin.

David Selby, head of Thomson Cruises, said last night: *'We delighted to announce that we are expanding our UK programme by adding Liverpool to our range of UK ports in 2008'*.

30 cruises, with 50,000 passengers, starting in Liverpool during 2008 to Amazon, Greenland and the Mediterranean is a record. A city council spokesman says: *'The new cruise liner facility is on course to be completed on time for the official launch in September, which will coincide with the arrival of the 'QE2' to Liverpool'*

Pontoons for the terminal will be attached to tugs in four sections and towed from Canada Dock, where they have been constructed and moved into place at Princes Dock. There they will be attached to piles which have been sunk into the river bed.

Council Leader Warren Bradley said: *'This latest move brings home the fact that the cruise liner terminal is becoming a reality. It is a vitally important development not only for the city but for the region and will have a huge impact on our future as a world city. Liverpool is an outward-looking, vibrant dynamic city which is attracting more and more visitors.*

'Already the confirmed bookings will bring in many thousands of passengers and we are still getting a huge amount of interest and enquiries from cruise companies all over the world.

And, of course, we will have the QE2 at the official launch of the facility in September.

'It has been very encouraging that it is largely local workers who are being used on this scheme.'

Steven Broomhead, of the Northwest Regional Development Agency said: *'More than 25 cruises are expected to be tying up in Liverpool each year by 2009 and that will bring a new influx of tourists for the region's outstanding tourist attractions while providing a boost to the economy.*

'With Capital of Culture fast approaching for Liverpool, the addition of a cruise liner facility will ensure that the infrastructure is in place to secure the city as an international destination for the future.'

The first liners are due to berth at the new terminal in September. The new terminal involves creating an extension connected to the existing landing stage at Princes Dock, allowing cruise ships of up to 350-metres in length to berth.

It's a massive boost to tourism, and brings home the fact that our cruise liner terminal is fast becoming a reality.

The terminal is a vitally important development not only for the city, but for the region and will have a huge impact on our future as a world city.

This means that once again the biggest liners in the world will be able to visit the Mersey on a regular basis. So we end the long procession of people and events which has created a Transatlantic bridge between Britain and the United States and made Liverpool the Gateway to America.

Appendix

Selected passages from the book written by a former Chaplain to Liverpool Seaman's Mission on the working conditions of seamen sailing between Liverpool and San Francisco in the late nineteenth century.

British Merchant Seamen in San Francisco - 1892 - 1896.

It can be shown that not only is there grounds for it, but that probably no class of men in this world have such deep cause for complaint as the men and boys who man the sailing-ships of Great Britain. It can also be shown that with a few alterations, entailing little trouble and trifling expense, the present causes of discontent could be largely removed.

It must be borne in mind that glorious or ignoble traditions have much to do with the esprit de corps of men and nations. The British Royal Navy has a long past of glorious deeds to nerve it for future trials and responsibilities.

The history of its past gives a moral strength and fibre to every officer, man and boy in it, whilst the improved conditions under which the men now live and receive their pay has made it the most popular service in England.

As a glorious past causes the present generation to thrill with the desire to repeat and add to the deeds of their ancestors, so the evil traditions connected with the merchant service – which are by no means ancient history – still have their influence on the minds of merchant seamen.

It is not many years ago since numbers of ships, leaky, overloaded, and not a few of them meant to sink – as Mr. Plimsoll stated – were sent to sea, which would probably have been the case still if he, for the simple sake of humanity, had not succeeded, against much opposition, in getting the load line marked on every British ship.

It is not many years since food of the cheapest sort, often really unfit for human consumption, was given to the sailors to eat. Visions of maggoty biscuits and stinking pork, of coloured water for coffee, which is still too frequently seen, of the barest of ' bare whack,' of horrible forecastles with the vilest ventilation and least possible light, of frequent use of belaying-pins and rope-ends, still pass before the minds of the merchant sailor.

They form much of the tradition upon which he has to feed, and do not, of course, act upon his character in the same way that the traditions of the navy do upon its men.

True, many of these things have been removed by a more enlightened age, and by the humanizing and moderating influences of the Board of Trade—although much more might yet be done in the way of improvement.

The voyage to San Francisco is a very long one, either taking four to six months round Cape Horn or taking two to three months round Australia.

If we can follow in our mind the path of a ship leaving England, with her mixed crew of men, her half-dozen or so of apprentices, petty officers and officers, some twenty-five to forty hands all told, we can more fully realize what pocket-money means to them in San Francisco.

Leaving the temperate climes of England, in three or four weeks they are in the intense heat of the equator, then on into the temperate clime again, and in another four weeks or so are in the gales, ice, snow, and mountainous seas off the Horn. Cape Horn may be rounded in a sea like the proverbial duck-pond, but as a rule beating out round the Horn is terrible work.

Not infrequently ships are kept there several weeks vainly trying to get round the Cape against continual gales, heavy seas and in winter terrible cold, often with the sails half frozen and the rigging and decks coated in ice.

Without doubt many a man and boy then learns what suffering means, and many a thought wings its way to a comfortable home far away in old England—its peace, quietness, and security— whilst here is the great ship stunning and crashing into the waste of waters off Cape Horn and the water swishing along the decks.

Hard it is—yea, harder than anyone knows—when soaked and half frozen with cold, after struggling perhaps for an hour or more out on yardarms with bellying and icy sails, with the ship rolling and plunging beneath, to come down from aloft, and have a hard biscuit to eat and some coloured hot water to drink for coffee!

After rounding the Horn and sailing for three weeks or so, the equator is again reached, and in two or three weeks the ship enters the great Bay of San Francisco. This voyage is not often accomplished under four months, usually four to six months.

It is hard for us who live on shore to realize what this means to young high-spirited men and boys, of whom there are always a very large number. They have been cooped up on the narrow limits of a ship's deck for a period of time extending from four to six months.

The crimps boarded the ship the moment of arrival, and all their tempting goods and chattels were laid out before the crew, and a number of the men were soon on the way to the shore with their 'friends and protectors'.

On the next morning the writer met six of those young sailors in the Seamen's Institute, and asked them how they possibly could have done such a mad act as to leave the ship with six months' pay due to them.

Their simple reply was that they were wretched in mind and body, with an intense desire to go ashore and have a good meal.

The crimps (a type of press gang member) were ready at hand to satisfy both these desires, and offer much more in addition.

Four of these sailors were badly touched with scurvy. They showed the writer their legs from the knee downwards, and they were much discoloured; moreover, their gums were affected.

The writer told them they were not fit to go to sea, and should be in the hospital, and said he would go at once to the British Consul, and arrange to get them sent there.

They replied they would have to see the boarding-master about it. Unfortunately, the writer did not ask their names, nor that of the house in which they were staying; but they promised, after seeing him, to come back, and wait at the Institute till they heard what the Consul said.

The matter was immediately reported to the British Consul, who promised to see the men attended to, and asked for them to be sent to him without delay.

The writer then returned to the Institute, but the sailors were not there. He never saw them again, and the next morning ascertained that those men, with scurvy upon them, were shipped away for another five months' voyage on a deep-water ship bound round the Horn, after being sixteen hours on shore from a voyage of about seven months!

The British Consul was in no way to blame. The abominable conditions under which sailors are shipped away, after being lured or starved out of their ships, are the cause of such monstrous occurrences.

That ship lay in San Francisco three months. The sail-maker on board, an old and most respectable man, fell ill.

He was taken to the hospital, and there he lay for about a fortnight, a perfect example of patience and resignation, and then, without much suffering, without a murmur, and only words of gratitude for those who attended him, that brave old sailor breathed his last, and was laid to rest thousands of miles from his home, his friends, and all he loved.

Many another case could be given of the great misery that comes too often to the apprentices who desert, and their very real regret that they ever took the step. Of the apprentices who deserted during the five years the writer spent among seamen in San Francisco, he only knows of one who prospered. Several of the others died miserable deaths, others sank into saloons, tobacco stores, and other places, whilst a number got places as conductors on the street cars, and spent the time which should have been occupied in learning their profession in collecting 5-cent car fares. The writer well remembers walking along Kearny Street one morning and seeing two shoeblacks making signs of recognition. They were two deserting apprentices who had been reduced to blacking boots to try and gain a livelihood. It could hardly be said that their prospects in life had improved.

Look at it how we will, desertion is a very serious thing to great numbers of sailors, and to a very large number of apprentices it is little less than a fatal blow to their prospects as a Merchant Navy officer.

It is easy for some to run down British sailors, call them a drunken lot, always making trouble, insubordinate, and profligate —statements which, by the way, are by no means correct—but before any class of men can be saluted with epithets such as these, we had better find out whether they are the subjects of fair play, honesty, and justice, or of poor food, insidious robbery through commission, and other means of oppression related in these pages.

When men are fairly and honestly fed and treated, they will often show a side to their character of willing obedience and contentment, which is never even so much as suspected by those who do not treat them fairly.

British seamen will not show the best side of their character when they are oppressed, but the worst We cannot be altogether surprised at this, as what is often called 'making trouble' on board a ship is merely refusing to endure in silence, a grievous wrong.

Discipline, and strict discipline, must be maintained, and it is very much more easily enforced when men are living and working under good and fair conditions of life than the opposite.

Not only for the comfort of the men themselves, but also for the welfare of the British nation, it must be fervently hoped that the conditions under which merchant seamen live on board ships may be so improved that men and boys of the British race may once more be found manning their own country's ships, doing their work contentedly and industriously, feeling that they are following a calling, hard at times though it be, which yet offers as many inducements in earning a livelihood as are presented to those who work on shore.

Revd. James Fell.

Acknowledgements

Except for general historical information, the primary facts in this publication were researched personally from public and private institutions, from Internet sources, and a number of individuals and Resource Centres.

In no particular order I would like to acknowledge and thank the following for their invaluable help in producing this book.

- Michael Otterson. Media and Communications Department. LDS (Mormon) Church Salt Lake City.
- David Murrant. Director Service Groups. Sony Computer Entertainment. USA.
- New York Times – Images from WW1.
- BBC Liverpool. Liverpool Jewish History.
- Cushing Memorial Library. Texas. Images and documents US Army Liverpool WW2.
- Ian Ralston. Lecturer. American Studies. Liverpool John Moores University.
- Mr & Mrs Ralph Boyd. USA. Information US Army Liverpool WW2.
- Aldon P Ferguson. Images and extracts from his book 'Lancashire Airfields in the Second World War'.
- Professor Peter Fearon. School of Historical Studies. University of Leicester.
- Tony Higginson of www.liverpoolauthors.com and Phil Finegan of Ribcar for their help and patience in the production of this book.
- Dr John Rowlands